RELIGIOUS POEMS

"The testimony of one Soul is the experience of thousands"—
for
"As in water face answereth to face, so the heart of man to man."
—PROVERBS 27:19.

Religious Poems

❦

BY
ELIZABETH PRENTISS
AUTHOR OF "STEPPING HEAVENWARD" AND "AUNT JANE'S HERO."

CURIOSMITH
MINNEAPOLIS

Published by Curiosmith.
Minneapolis, Minnesota.
Internet: curiosmith.com.

Previously published by Anson D. F. Randolph & Company in 1873.

Supplementary content, book layout, and cover design:
Copyright © 2017 Charles J. Doe

ISBN 9781946145338

CONTENTS

1. THE BATTLE OF LIFE . . . 9

2. THANKSGIVING . . . 11

3. THE GLADNESS OF MY JOY . . . 12

4. CHRIST VICTORIOUS . . . 13

5. THE WAY HOME . . . 14

6. CHRIST EVERYWHERE . . . 16

7. THE PERFECT FRIEND . . . 17

8. CHRIST'S INVITATION . . . 18

9. A PRAYER . . . 20

10. GOD KNOWS . . . 21

11. A SONG TO CHRIST . . . 23

12. THE BITTER CUP . . . 24

13. LIFE'S PROMISES . . . 25

14. MORE LOVE TO THEE, O CHRIST . . . 26

15. TO BE LIKE THEE . . . 27

16. CHOOSE . . . 28

17. NO IDLE WING . . . 29

18. A PRAYER . . . 30

19. COME HOME! . . . 32

20. "LORD, WHAT WOULDST THOU HAVE ME TO DO?" . . . 33

21. SEEKING THE WATER-BROOKS . . . 35

22. THE PRODIGAL . . . 36

23. A PRAYER . . . 38

24. THE MYSTERY OF LIFE IN CHRIST . . . 39

25. LOVING CHRIST FOR HIMSELF ALONE . . . 40

26. "MY CUP RUNNETH OVER" . . . 41

27. HOLD ME UP . . . 42

28. THE SAFE PLACE . . . 43

29. THE NEW SONG . . . 45

30. CONFESSION . . . 46

31. THE POWER OF CHRIST . . . 47

32. LOVE TO CHRIST . . . 48

33. THE BROKEN WING . . . 49

34. GOD IS FOR ME . . . 51

35. FESTAL DAYS . . . 52

36. SPEAK OF CHRIST . . . 53
37. NOT FIT TO GO . . . 55
38. WITH GREAT DELIGHT . . . 56
39. OH COME TO CHRIST . . . 57
40. THEY HAVE BEEN WITH JESUS . . . 58
41. THE FRIEND OF THE LONELY . . . 59
42. UNDER THE ROD . . . 60
43. THE WORK OF PEACE . . . 61
44. WHY EMPTY AND SAD? . . . 62
45. REST . . . 63
46. CHRIST ON THE SHORE . . . 64
47. AT CHRIST'S TABLE . . . 66
48. IS THE HEART READY? . . . 67
49. "GOD IS HERE" . . . 68
50. THE SCHOOL . . . 70
51. MY KINDRED . . . 72
52. CHRIST ASKS FOR ALL . . . 73
53. THE UNSEEN SPIRIT . . . 74
54. A PRAYER FOR CHARITY . . . 75
55. AT JESUS' FEET . . . 76
56. A STEADFAST HEART . . . 77
57. DEATH . . . 78
58. GOD'S SAINTS . . . 79
59. MY EXPECTATION IS FROM THEE . . . 80
60. WHAT CHRIST CAN BE . . . 81
61. THE SEA OF FIRE . . . 83
62. STAYING THERE—COMING BACK . . . 84
63. DRAW NEARER! . . . 85
64. "AND YE ARE CHRIST'S" . . . 86
65. WHEREIN TO GLORY . . . 87
66. "IS IT WELL WITH THE CHILD?" . . . 88
67. "IS IT WELL WITH THEE?" . . . 89
68. GO AND TELL JESUS . . . 90
69. A WISH . . . 91
70. HEALING . . . 92
71. WEARINESS . . . 93

72. THE ORANGE-TREE . . . 94
73. EVER AT WORK . . . 95
74. BACKSLIDING . . . 96
75. SO BE IT . . . 97
76. "NEARER TO THEE" . . . 98
77. NIGHT . . . 99
78. REST . . . 100
79. FAINT NOT . . . 101
80. NOT POOR . . . 102
81. IN GRIEF AND SHAME . . . 103
82. "IN REMEMBRANCE OF ME" . . . 104
83. "HE MUST INCREASE, BUT I MUST DECREASE" . . . 105
84. NEARER TO CHRIST . . . 107
85. WALKING WITH GOD . . . 108
86. A CUP OF WATER . . . 109
87. ANGELS' FOOD . . . 110
88. TESTIMONY . . . 111
89. "AT EVENING TIME THERE SHALL BE LIGHT" . . . 112
90. A COLD HEART . . . 113
91. SATISFIED . . . 114
92. "MY GOLDEN HOURS" . . . 115
93. THE GIFT . . . 116
94. JOINT HEIR WITH CHRIST . . . 118
95. GOD'S WAY . . . 120
96. PRAYER . . . 121
97. WHERE IS HE? . . . 122
98. THE MOTHER . . . 123
99. "OH, COME THOU DOWN TO ME, OR TAKE ME UP TO THEE!" . . . 125
100. "DYING, YET BEHOLD WE LIVE" . . . 126
101. ONLY JESUS . . . 128
102. "YOUR DARLING SLEEPS" . . . 129
103. NEARER . . . 131
104. SORROW . . . 132
105. "GOD LONGS TO BE LONGED FOR, HE LOVES TO BE SOUGHT" . . . 134

CONTENTS (continued)

106. BROKEN TO BE MENDED . . . 135
107. "THAT I MAY WIN CHRIST" . . . 136
108. AN ANGEL SMILING . . . 137
109. YEARNING . . . 138
110. THE CHRISTIAN LIFE . . . 139
111. HE IS MINE . . . 140
112. "AM I MY BROTHER'S KEEPER?" . . . 142
113. ALONE WITH GOD . . . 143
114. IT CANNOT LAST . . . 144
115. SOMETHING FOR CHRIST . . . 145
116. FORGIVE! . . . 147
117. THE PILGRIM . . . 148
118. WORK . . . 150
119. JESUS, BE ALL . . . 151
120. COMPLETE IN CHRIST . . . 152
121. "JOY UNSPEAKABLE" . . . 153
122. THE CRY OF THE YOUNG WIFE . . . 155

APPENDIX
"NEW YEAR THOUGHTS" from "The Sabbath at Home" . . . 161
REPLY OF THE NEW YEAR . . . 164

THE BATTLE OF LIFE

The wintry storm was raging loud without,
    And to and fro,
The angry winds flung carelessly about,
    The falling snow.

Luxuriously before the ruddy fire
    I sat at ease,
The only object of my heart's desire
    Myself to please.

A voice aroused me from my idle dreams;
    "Rise, rise, my child!
Shake thyself loose from these unfruitful schemes,
    These fancies wild.

"Come forth with me, and buffet wind and storm
    And icy cold;
Come as thou art, nor stay thy shrinking form
    Thus to enfold!"

It was the Master's voice. I could but yield
    To its behest,
While dread repugnance lay but ill concealed
    Within my breast.

Behind me closed my sheltering door; I faced
    The tempest rude;
Wild, savage winds my shrinking form embraced
    While thus I stood

Upon the threshold, casting longing eyes
    Back to my home,
Reluctant from my childhood's Paradise
    Enforced to roam.

Then plunging onward towards th' appointed way,
    I madly went,
And night and day, yea, many a night and day,
    My figure bent

Beneath the blast. Assailed with shudderings dire,
    By fears opprest,

Despairing, hopeless, stript of all desire,
  I onward prest.
Until I heard above the thunder's roll
  The Master's voice
Arise once more. It cried: "Oh, faithless soul,
  Behold thy choice!

"A life-long childhood, basking idly on
  The lap of ease,
Or manhood's strength by long endurance won
  In toils like these.

"Whether to gird thyself to walk with Me
  Mid conflicts dread,
Or back effeminate to ease to flee—
  Living—yet dead."

Already by my labors stronger grown,
  I stood and cried:
"Master and Lord! with Thee, with Thee alone,
  Let me abide.

"Let me but know I buffet wind and storm,
  With Thee, with Thee!
Upon my path Thine own divinest form
  But let me see!"

Thus in the hour of battle choice was made!
  Choice of unrest!
Thus Christian manhood seeking, undismayed
  The storm I breast.

No leisure now, no dreams, no idle time;
  I wrestle on;
Beat, icy winds, oppose, oh adverse clime,
  Till victory's won.

For I shall win! I shall come forth at last
  Not lost, but found!
A Christian warrior whom each stormy blast
  Hath victor crowned!

THANKSGIVING

I thank Thee, O my God, that through Thy grace
   I know Thee, who Thou art;
That I have seen the beauty of Thy face
   And felt Thee in my heart.

I thank Thee, O my Saviour, who hast deigned
   To stoop to even me;
Within my inmost soul hast ruled and reigned,
   And will my ransom be.

I thank Thee, Holy Spirit, that Thy wings
   Brood o'er my wandering mind;
Bringing to my remembrance sacred things
   To which my eyes were blind.

I thank Thee, Triune God! But oh, how cold
   The warmest words I speak;
For love and goodness strange and manifold,
   All human words are weak.

O teach me, then, to praise Thee with my life;
   With stern obedience;
To make the atmosphere about me rife
   With silent eloquence!

THE GLADNESS OF MY JOY

Thou art "the gladness of my joy."

The world has varied charms, yet none
    Without some base alloy,
I turn from it to Thee, my God,
    The gladness of my joy.

Sorrow may sorely press me down,
    Yet not my peace destroy,
It only drives my soul to Thee,
    Still gladness of my joy.

Earth's highest prize becomes a straw,
    A worthless, glittering toy,
Beside Thy beauty, O my God,
    The gladness of my joy.

Then let me all my heart and soul,
    My every power employ,
In serving, praising Thee, who art
    The gladness of my joy.

CHRIST VICTORIOUS

Oh, days of sickness, grief and pain,
What bring ye in your mournful train?
Grey hairs, old age before its time—
The breaking down of manhood's prime,
The trembling hand, the fainting heart,
Bruises and wounds to throb and smart,
The nerve unstrung, the sleepless brain;
Oh, these come boldly in your train.

But days of sickness, grief and pain,
Do these alone make up your train?
Not so! not so! The ranks between
Submission's gracious form is seen;
And with the boldest of the band
Sweet Patience ventures hand in hand,
While Faith, Christ's honor to maintain
Rides, dauntless, mid your hostile train.

Come, then, wild troop of griefs and pains
And riot on my Lord's domains!
Where you lay waste, another Hand
A firmer fabric long has planned;
What you destroy, Faith's radiant smile
Declares is for a little while;
And Christ himself shall come to reign
Victorious o'er your helpless train.

THE WAY HOME

A stranger in a foreign land, bewildered and astray,
I sought a guide sagacious to point me out the way—
    The nearest way home.

My hand in his enclasping, he led me by his side,
Through thickets and through brambles, into a desert wide,
    A weary way home!

Other pilgrims thronged the path, but not one of them I knew,
They eyed me with suspicion, or with greetings cold and few;
    Ah, lonely way home!

Despondent sank my heart, weary grew my toiling brain,
In the throng and in the darkness I strained my eyes in vain
    To see the way home.

At last the silence breaking, "Are we almost there?" I cried;
"I am weary, breathless, lonely, yet we wander far and wide
    From my own dear home!"

Then gently on my ear fell the answer grave and sweet,
"The way thou art traversing bears the print of thousand feet
    By me guided home.

"On these rocks they well-nigh slipped, on these sands were parched
    and faint;
Every mountain-pass has echoed to the sound of their complaint,
    On the hard way home.

"Few were the faithful hearts that their guide distrusted not,
That held their peace, pressed onward, and the lonely way forgot,
    In the blissful thought of home.

"But when the blessed vision, through Him at last attained,
Broke on their longing sight as the mountain-top was gained,
    And they saw the lost home,

"Every one, straightway forgetting all the perils, all the fears,
All the struggles, faintings, conflicts of the fast receding years,
    Kissed the hand that led home!"

He spoke, and with a smile full of tenderness and love,
He raised his hand and pointed to the sunny heights above,
    And I saw, I saw home!

Then with mingled joy and shame, with contrition sad and sweet,
I bathed with tears repentant those travel-wounded feet,
    That led me to my home.

And patient now press onward, the stony path ascend,
Every hour drawing nearer to the painful journey's end—
    Almost home! almost home!

CHRIST EVERYWHERE

To Zion's gates, where holy hearts are meeting,
My eager footsteps thankfully repair;
My soul, expectant, waits a joyful greeting,
For Christ, Himself, is there.

Unto my closet gladly I betake me,
Driven by sorrow, weariness and care;
Ah, what a blessed suppliant they make me,
For Christ, my Lord, is there.

Sick-rooms, and broken hearts, and dying pillows,
With mournful voices fill the silent air;
Thither I go, for walking on life's billows,
The risen Christ is there.

And every day I hasten to my calling,
Facing, with fearless heart, temptation's snare;
The world's enticements cease to be appalling,
Since Christ is always there.

And so, when life's brief daylight hours are ending,
And Death, defiant, urges to despair,
Strong in immortal hope, my soul ascending,
Shall answer, Christ is there!

THE PERFECT FRIEND

Lord, from myself, my faults, my sins
    Heart-sick, to Thee I flee!
With each new day anew begins
    Folly's supremacy.

And from my dearest friends I fly—
    They err, they change, they fail;
My hopes they disappoint; well-nigh
    My faith in man assail.

To Thee I come! *Thou* canst not sin;
    I come to Thee for rest!
Oh, let a weary wanderer in,
    By sin and grief opprest!

Looking to Thee, Lord, day by day,
    Let me myself forget,
Meekly content to let Thee pay,
    Dear Lord, of sin my debt.

Looking to Thee with all the love
    Once to earth's treasures given,
Content to find, at last, above,
    Perfected friends in heaven!

CHRIST'S INVITATION

I.

Press close, my child, to Me,
  Closer to Me;
Earth hath no resting-place
  Ready for thee!
Straight to my shelter flee,
Press close, my child, to Me,
  Closer to Me!

II.

Love, pleasure, riches, fame,
  All may be thine,
And the immortal soul
  Still will repine;
I must be all to thee,
Press close, my child, to Me,
  Closer to Me.

III.

Life may for thee contend,
  Hard toil and care
Strive to divide from Me,
  Crowd everywhere;
Let them my servants be—
Press thee, my child, to Me,
  Closer to Me.

IV.

Grief of thy heart may make
  A desert drear,
Yet there my suff'rers learn
  My voice to hear,
Calling, with earnest plea,
Press close, my child, to Me,
  Closer to Me.

V.

Come, then, my child to Me,

Make thyself Mine;
I give Myself to thee,
I will be Thine.
Joy, grief and care shall be
Thus binding thee to Me,
Closer to Me.

A PRAYER

Oh, Strongest of the strong! Be Thou the stay
Of the weak creature that Thy hand has made;
I am so helpless that each moment brings
Some new, some pressing reason for Thine aid.

Oh, Wisest of the wise! I nothing know,
I am so ignorant, so poor, so blind!
Be Thou my Teacher, be my Light, my Guide,
Show me the pathway that I cannot find.

Oh, Kindest of the kind! I come to Thee
Longing for favors that I sorely need;
Open Thy bounteous hand, for Thou art He
Whose choice it is to give, in word and deed.

Oh, Truest of the true! When others fail,
Thy years remain the same; be it my lot
To share Thy faithful friendship! Dearest Lord,
Mid human changes, oh, forget me not!

Oh, Gentlest of the gentle! Speak one word
And give one smile, one single smile to me;
No voice is soft as Thine, no earthly smile
So beautiful, so ravishing can be.

Oh, Best among the good! Make me like Thee!
Strong, wise and kind in attributes divine,
True, gentle, good, in graces not of earth—
Let me in Thy reflected beauty shine.

GOD KNOWS

I.

Thou knowest them that trust in Thee!
   What precious words, O Lord, are these!
Here let Thy suffering children flee,
   When struggling mid life's mysteries!

II.

For to our childish minds, Thy will
   Looks ofttimes hard, and passing strange;
Loving, we doubt and fear Thee still,
   And long Thy wondrous ways to change.

III.

Not thus we cry, would we assail
   That saintly soul with blow on blow;
Not thus should Sorrow, stern and pale,
   Put forth her hand and lay him low.

IV.

What needs he, Lord, of pain and smart?
   To Thee is he not consecrate?
His joy, his hope, his all, Thou art,
   Ever on Thee he loves to wait.

V.

Ah, dearest Lord, Thou knowest best!
   Thou knowest them that trust in Thee!
Blessed the soul, yea, doubly blest,
   When Thou dost try its constancy.

VI.

Upon the soft and crumbling stone,
   The sculptor spends a passing hour;
He strikes immortal blows alone
   When chiselled marble feels his power.

VII.

And when the ore is rich and rare
   The miner strikes and strikes again;

Labor and toil he need not spare,
    He never can exhaust the vein.

VIII.

Thou knowest, Lord, a stone to choose—
    Worthy the labor of Thy hand;
Thou fearest not the tool to use
    That gives it shape at Thy command.

IX.

Thou knowest many a hidden mine
    Where Thou canst enter at Thy will;
Treasures of faith therein are thine,
    Worthy of e'en the Master's skill.

X.

Ah, Lord! we will not stay Thy hand
    With folly's questions, folly's fears;
Thy ways we cannot understand—
    Forgive our weakness and our tears.

XI.

Move on in Thy mysterious way,
    We'll stand aside Thy work to see;
Faithful the work, and blessed they,
    Who cannot trace, but trust in Thee.

A SONG TO CHRIST

As on a vast, eternal shore,
   The waves unceasing roll,
So He whom all the worlds adore
   Blesses thy soul, oh child of earth,
     Blesses thy human soul.

Then roll thou back in tidal waves
   Thanksgivings to His name;
Sing Christ, sing Christ, who loves and saves,
   Who built thy mortal frame, my soul,
     Who built thy mortal frame.

Day follows day, night follows night;
   And ever on their wings
Christ sends thee joy and peace and light;
   Each hour new blessings brings, my heart,
     Each hour new blessings brings.

Then let each day become a song,
   And every night a hymn;
Each hour the song, the hymn prolong,
   Till tears thine eyes bedim, thrice blest!
     Till tears thine eyes bedim.

Count up thy mercies, child of clay—
   Recount them o'er and o'er;
Yet canst thou tell, in life's short day,
   The sands upon the shore, oh child?
     The sands upon the shore?

Nay, then, but thou in heaven shalt sing,
   Sing songs to Christ for aye;
Exultant shall thy praises ring
   Through an eternal day, glad heart,
     Through an eternal day!

THE BITTER CUP

"The cup that my Father has given me, shall I not drink it?"

I.

I take the cup, my Father, from Thy hand;
    Its every drop was measured out by Thee;
How to bring healing Thou dost understand,
    Who only knowest my soul's malady.
Quick, let me drink this draught at Thy behest,
Drink it for speedy healing, speedy rest.

II.

Nay then, Thou will'st not so! But sip by sip
    Must I its bitterness disheartened taste;
Today, tomorrow, press it to my lip,
    Careful that not a single drop I waste;
And while my human soul for cordial begs,
Must drink this draught revolting to its dregs.

III.

What then? Shall I, who go to drink with Thee,
    New wine in the dear Kingdom of Thy Son,
Shrink from the cup this life holds out to me,
    Asking, with coward heart, a sweeter one?
Have I not owned myself diseased and faint,
And of my poor soul-sickness made complaint?

IV.

Give me the cup, my Master! See me clasp
    With willing hands, this remedy from Thine!
Forgive the mortal shudder, mortal gasp
    That proves me human, proves me not divine;
Slowly each drop I'll taste, and one by one;
For Thee I drink, Lord, let Thy will be done!

LIFE'S PROMISES

Oh human life, thy promises are sweet,
   They fall upon the ear
In cadence charming, and their tones repeat
   In accents clear.

But dost thou keep thy promise? Can I trust
   Thy silvery voice,
Will it awaken echo-tones that must
   Bid me rejoice?

Ah no! one voice alone my soul hath heard
   That ne'er deceived,
One Heart alone the depths of mine has stirred,
   Yet never grieved.

Jesus, I turn to Thee! oh let me hide
   Within thy breast,
Refuge and shelter, peace and grace provide,
   And needed rest.

For in the mazes of a troublous hour
   I make my way;
Oh come to me, Thou hast the will, the power,
   Be mine alway!

MORE LOVE TO THEE, O CHRIST

I.

More love to Thee, O Christ,
  More love to Thee!
Hear Thou the prayer I make
  On bended knee:
This is my earnest plea—
More love, O Christ, to Thee,
  More love to Thee!

II.

Once earthly joy I craved,
  Sought peace and rest,
Now Thee alone I seek,
  Give what is best:
This all my prayer shall be—
More love, O Christ, to Thee,
  More love to Thee!

III.

Let sorrow do its work,
  Send grief and pain,
Sweet are Thy messengers,
  Sweet their refrain,
When they can sing with me—
More love, O Christ, to Thee,
  More love to Thee!

IV.

Then shall my latest breath
  Whisper Thy praise,
This be the parting cry
  My heart shall raise:
This still its prayer shall be—
More love, O Christ, to Thee,
  More love to Thee!

TO BE LIKE THEE

Oh Jesus Christ, in self-despair
I come to Thee! Hear Thou the prayer
Laid at Thy feet; I leave it there—
    To be like Thee!

Turn out the darling bosom-sin,
The love of self that rules within,
My earnest longing let me win—
    To be like Thee!

O let me see Thy lovely face,
O let me hear Thy words of grace,
In Thine own image grow apace—
    To be like Thee!

O Gentle, Sinless, Undefiled,
Ev'n in Thy Justice meek and mild,
Help me, Thy loving, longing child—
    To be like Thee!

CHOOSE

I.

Now choose my heart!
From Jesus wilt thou part?
Because an earthly friend
Would thee attend?

II.

What can earth give
That will untarnished live?
Hast thou found any rest
Save on Christ's breast?

III.

Think of the price
The precious sacrifice
That Jesus paid for thee,
And to Him flee.

IV.

Thou dost still wait?
Dost dare to hesitate?
Lord Jesus make this heart
From idols part.

V.

Hanging on Thee
From all else let it flee,
Before Thee let it fall
Its All in All.

NO IDLE WING

Oh do not let a single day go by
    On idle wings, without some loving word,
Some loving deed, from my blest heart, for Thee,
    Who art my Saviour, art my risen Lord!
For Thou for me hast all things done and said;
    Hast paid my debts, hast intercession made,
When crushed with sense of weakness and of sin,
    To plead my cause with Thee I was afraid.

I know not why, I dare not ask Thee why,
    Thou hast been pleased to give such gifts to me;
It was the out-growth of no grace of mine,
    For I had nought but sins to offer Thee.
Sins? Ah, there are not words enough to tell
    How complicate, how manifold were they!
How long I tried Thy patience, and how far
    My restless footsteps led from Thee astray.

But Thou hast lured me back, and lo I come,
    Longing to do Thy will! oh make it plain,
And let my grateful life flow forth in waves
    That shall bear many a treasure to the main.
Bear them, yet know it not, as the deep sea,
    Wots not what riches float upon its breast,
Content to ebb and flow beneath Thine eye,
    To ebb and flow simply at Thy behest.

A PRAYER

Lord, I am weary of myself,
    Let me more weary be,
Stay not Thy hand until I learn
    From it for aye to flee,
And all that I have loved, to pour
    In lavish floods, on Thee.

Do not I leap for joy, when saints
    To praise Thy name combine?
Is not Thy name a sweeter sound
    Than this poor name of mine?
Do I love better to be praised
    Than to hear praise of Thine?

Alas! two passions strong and deep,
    Contend my soul within,
I love myself, but I love Thee,
    And long Thy grace to win,
Long to be like Thee, to get free
    From the old life of sin.

Which of the twain shall win the day?
    Oh empty out this heart,
Dwell there in peace and leave not self
    In its remotest part—
I want to yield it all to Thee
    Who its dear Master art.

I want to be all eye, all ear,
    Jesus, for Thee alone,
To be forgotten, lost, cast out,
    Knowing, but all unknown,
To feel Thee sitting as my King
    On undisputed throne.

This is my feeble prayer, oh hear
    My poor, my childish cry,
Do for me what I cannot do,

And pass in mercy by.
I have not courage self to slay,
Do Thou then make it die.

COME HOME!

"My suffering child! Thy days of grief are o'er,
Come home to Me, and rest for evermore."

Jesus! Thou Lord of all! I dare not go;
No work well done for Thee I have to show.

"Great deeds I ask not; but some act of love,
One word for Me thy righteousness may prove."

Alas! I do remember no such word,
Nor one such act! Pardon me, oh my Lord!

"Yet come, my child, 'tis I who bid thee come,
Nothing I ask from thee; come home, come home!"

I cannot, dare not! Call me not Thy child,
Behold my hands, my heart, with sin defiled!
Behold my wasted life, my barren years,
Behold my murmurs, my rebellious tears;
See how myself I love while cold towards Thee,
My conscience seared, my hardened heart, oh see!

"I see. And since thou nought hast done for Me,
I have done all, poor, sorrowing soul, for thee;
The word that thou for me hast never spoken,
That word I spake for thee with faith unbroken;
The loving deed thou didst not, I have done,
And interceded for thee near the throne.
Thy sins, thy wasted life, thy heart defiled,
Better I know than thou dost know them, child,
And freely all that sin I have forgiven;
Come home, my child, come home to Me and heaven."

My blessed Lord! My Saviour and my All!
Weeping no longer, I obey Thy call,
I come, to praise Thee with my heart and voice,
I come, with blood-bought sinners to rejoice;
I bless my dying day, I bless the grace
That gives me with Thy ransomed ones a place.
Now for eternity that grace to see,
Now for eternal songs to sing to Thee!

"LORD, WHAT WOULDST THOU HAVE ME TO DO?"

Hast Thou, my Master, aught for me to do
    To honor Thee today?
Hast thou a word of love to some poor soul,
    That I may say?

For see, this world that Thou hast made so fair,
    Within its heart is sad;
Thousands are lonely, thousands sigh and weep;
    But few are glad.

To which of them shall I stretch forth my hand,
    With sympathetic grasp?
Whose fainting form, for Thy dear sake, shall I
    Fondly enclasp?

They all are dear to Thee; and loving Thee,
    Dear are they all to me;
In every visage marred by grief and pain,
    Thy mark I see.

Straight from my heart, each day a blessing goes
    Warmly, through Thee, to theirs;
They are enfolded in my inmost soul,
    And in my prayers.

But which, among them all, is mine *today?*
    O guide my willing feet,
To some poor soul that fainting on the way
    Needs counsel sweet.

Or into some sick-room, where I may speak
    With tenderness of Thee;
And showing who and what Thou art, oh Christ,
    Bid sorrow flee.

Or unto one whose straits call not for words;
    To one in want, in need;
Who will not counsel, but will take from me
    A loving deed.

Surely Thou hast some work for me to do!
Oh, open Thou mine eyes,
To see how Thou wouldst choose to have it done,
And where it lies!

SEEKING THE WATER-BROOKS

Hunted o'er valley, o'er plain and o'er mountain,
  Refuge none finding, relentless his foes;
Panteth the hart for the brook and the fountain,
  Panteth and thirsteth, nor seeks for repose.

Hunted, oh hunted this weary world over
  Refuge none finding my God, save in thee,
Thus pants my soul Thine abode to discover,
  Thus stretches onward Thy glory to see.

Sorrow, temptation and sin fast pursuing,
  Seek for my soul, for its ruin and death,
Onward I fly, my weak forces renewing,
  Thirsting and fainting and panting for breath.

Dry is the land, is my soul's lamentation;
  Thirsting and panting, fast onward I flee,
Fleeing from sorrow and sin and temptation,
  Thirsting and panting, Oh God! after Thee!

THE PRODIGAL

Into the Master's house my feet were led;
    An outcast's feet;
I drank the wine, tasted the living bread
    For angels meet.

Not as a servant did I waiting stand,
    For, wondrous grace!
Child of the house, I clasped the Master's hand
    And saw his face.

Yet, with a child's caprice, I learned to dread
    That form divine;
Tasteless became the true, the living bread,
    Tasteless the wine.

Wild longings seized me with resistless might;
    I stole away
And in the wilderness passed night by night
    And day by day.

Oh, weary nights! oh, days of sin and shame!
    Remorseful tears
Ooze from my heart, yearning to wash your name
    Off long past years!

Foot-sore, repentant, Master! unto Thee
    I crept once more—
More sinful, more forlorn, more foul to see,
    I gained Thy door.

Not as a child, but as a servant, Lord,
    I ventured nigh;
Trembling and waiting for a single word,
    Watching Thine eye;

Knowing I could give nothing for Thy grace,
    Do nought for Thee—
Still, still, I yearned to look upon Thy face,
    Look once—and flee!

And lingering thus, my Master heard my groans,
    Drew gently nigh,
Pity and pardon in His gracious tones,
    Peace in His eye.

Trembling, into His house once more my feet
    Were safely led;
Once more re-placed upon my Master's seat
    I broke His bread.

Of bitter memories by Love beguiled,
    I sat His guest:
Dear Lord! of thy repentant, trusting child
    Thou knowest the rest.

A PRAYER

I.

I love Thee, my Saviour! I love Thee! I love Thee!
Strong as a rock is my faith in Thy name;
Nought upon earth I desire above Thee;
My Joy and my Solace, my Hope and my Aim!

II.

I love Thee! But oh, with a limited measure;
I trust Thee! But oh, I'm ashamed of my trust;
I call Thee my All, and I seek for a treasure
That lies mid life's turmoil, and gleams from its dust.

III.

Oh, give me a love that the depths of my being
Shall stir into life that it never has known;
Love mighty in purpose, unselfish, far-seeing,
Grasping and proving to make me its own.

IV.

Give me a faith that shall ask Thee no question,
Shudder and shrink at no trial by fire;
Faith that is patient, that makes no suggestion,
Thou its sole Object, its single Desire!

V.

Urge me to seek Thee! Impel me, allure me!
Penetrate down to the depths of my soul;
Thou whose vast pity alone can endure me,
Take me, oh take me—the whole, Lord the whole!

VI.

Oh how I hate all my follies and seemings!
Loathe my self-love, my mistakes, and my sins;
Strength I have wasted in pitiful dreamings;
Nursing of fancies and petty chagrins!

VII.

Oh Thou All-Seeing, All-Loving, All-Knowing,
Penitent, weeping I lie at thy feet!
Take Thou this heart, with thy love it is glowing;
Take this whole life that Thy faith has made sweet!

THE MYSTERY OF LIFE IN CHRIST

I.

I walk along the crowded streets, and mark
    The eager, anxious faces;
Wondering what this man seeks, what that heart craves,
        In earthly places.

II.

Do I want any thing that they are wanting?
    Is each of them my brother?
Could we hold fellowship, speak heart to heart,
        Each to the other?

III.

Nay, but I know not! only this I know,
    That sometimes merely crossing
Another's path, where life's tumultuous waves
        Are ever tossing,

IV.

He, as he passes, whispers in mine ear
    One magic sentence only,
And in the awful loneliness of crowds
        I am not lonely.

V.

Ah, what a life is theirs who live in Christ;
    How vast the mystery!
Reaching in height to heaven, and in its depth
        The unfathomed sea!

LOVING CHRIST FOR HIMSELF ALONE

I.

I loved Thee once for what Thou wert to me,
God of my life and Saviour of my soul;
    I loved to roll
The burden of my safety upon Thee.

II.

I loved Thy gifts, and held them as Thy trust;
Looked at them often, clasped them to my heart;
    But would not part
At Thy behest, with one, save as I must.

III.

I loved myself, and through myself I tried
To see Thy beauty, and behold Thy face;
    Yet had not grace,
To cast this medium dim in scorn aside.

IV.

I love Thee now, oh Christ! for what Thou art,
Love Thy perfections and Thy name adore,
    Recount them o'er,
And at Thy feet lay down a thankful heart.

V.

And still I love Thy gifts, and know them all
To be kind tokens from my gracious Lord;
    But at a word
Will give them back to Thee at Thy recall.

VI.

And still I love myself,—alas, too well,
Yet do not see Thee through this glass defiled;
    Thy blessed child
Beholds Thy face, doth in Thy presence dwell.

VII.

Oh where are words to tell the joy unpriced
Of the rich heart, that breasting waves no more,
    Drifts thus to shore,
Laden with peace, and tending unto Christ!

"MY CUP RUNNETH OVER"

Jesus, I fain would sing a sweeter song
Than my glad heart has ever sung before;
For Thou, who hast been bountiful to me,
Hast filled my cup till it is running o'er.

Why hast Thou thus revealed Thyself to me?
Why hast Thy secret unto me made known?
Why singled me from many loving hearts,
Whispering these mysteries to me alone?

Thou art too good, too great, too wise, too kind;
And even while to see Thee I entreat,
My weakness puts Thee from me, and I cry
This is too great a joy, a bliss too sweet.

Oh stay Thine hand! I cannot, cannot bear
This weight of glory; cannot live, and see
The face that Thou in tender grace hast turned
On me, a sinful creature, even me.

Yes, I can bear Thy strokes, but not Thy love;
I can endure Thy frowns, but not Thy smile;
Frowns I deserve, and stripes I sorely need,
And Thine own choice has given them erewhile.

And yet amid my tears, my heart rings out
A richer song than songs it sang before;
For Thou who hast been bountiful to me,
Hast given a cup today that runneth o'er!

HOLD ME UP

"Hold Thou me up and I shall be safe."

I cannot trust myself, Jesus my Lord,
    Hold Thou me up!
My feet had well nigh slipped, with Thine own word
    Hold Thou me up!
Oh teach me how, and when, and where to go,
The path of safety I entreat to know.

I cannot walk alone; I am a child,
    Hold Thou me up;
And yet to try my strength am oft beguiled;
    Hold Thou me up!
Support me, lead me, keep me in Thy way
Be Thou my Surety, Thou my Strength and Stay.

Oh do not let me fall! I cling to Thee;
    Hold Thou me up;
Be merciful in this great strait to me,
    Hold Thou me up!
Let Thy strong hand prevent me; let Thy grace
Carry me safely past this slippery place.

For I have fallen, and I know its pain;
    Hold thou me up;
Fallen and risen, ris'n to fall again;
    Hold Thou me up;
My weakness and my helplesness I know;
Hold Thou me up, I will not let Thee go!

THE SAFE PLACE

I.

I went to Jesus with a prayer
    Upon a suppliant's knee;
Low at His Cross I laid me down,
    Nor asked His face to see,
Yet whispered in His ear the tale
    No mortal ear could bear;
The story of a faithless heart;
    And of its self-despair.

II.

I told Him how my feet had slipped;
    How often gone astray;
How oft my heart refused to love,
    My lips refused to pray.
In stammering words that none but He
    Hearing could understand,
I made complaint of careless work
    Done by a careless hand.

III.

Of wasted hours, of idle words,
    Of love oft waxing dim,
Of silence when a warmer heart
    Had testified of Him.
I owned my weak and selfish ways;
    How often all day long,
Moanings and sighs had filled His ears
    To whom I owed a song.
And what said He? What whispered words
    Responded unto mine?
Did He reproach me? Did His love
    On me refuse to shine?

IV.

Nay, thus He spake, and bent Him low
    To reach my anxious ear,
"My child, thou doest well to lie

As thou art lying here;
I *knew* thy human weakness, knew
Each lurking bosom-sin,
Knew it, and yet in loving grace
Thy heart I stooped to win.

V.

"I knew that thou would'st often fall,
Poor work for Me would'st do,
Would'st give me only half thy love,
Give praises faint and few.
And yet I chose thee. Be content;
And since thou canst not fly
To heights by dearer souls attained,
Let it suffice to lie

VI.

"Here at My feet; it is the place
To which My loved ones flee;
They find it sweet, and so shalt thou:
'Tis a safe place for thee."
Yes, it *is* sweet, and it is safe!
And here will I abide;
Sinful, and yet forgiven, sad,
And yet so satisfied!

THE NEW SONG

"And they sang a new Song."

There is a song I want to sing—
 Or want to learn to sing;
It is a song of praise to Thee,
 Jesus, my Lord and King.

Oh teach me all its varied notes,
 Its hidden melody,
Till I have learned to sing by heart,
 This song of praise to Thee.

I want to sing, while yet on earth,
 The tender, thankful strain
Of saints, who gladly near Thy throne,
 Make Thee their song's refrain.

For though I am not yet a saint,
 And though my praises ring
From an encumbered, earthly soul,
 I love the strains they sing.

And well I love, I know I love,
 Though truly not as they,
Thee, blessed Jesus whom I praise
 Feebly on earth today;

While there's a song I want to sing—
 Or want to learn to sing;
A blessed song of love to Thee,
 Jesus, my Lord and King.

CONFESSION

Jesus, is there a spot where I can hide
    To be alone with Thee,
Where I can whisper in Thy listening ear
    My earnest plea?

Oh I do long so to be sanctified;
    To be emancipate
From fellowship with evil, and to feel
    Of sin no weight.

Surely I love Thee;—and yet, if I do—
    Whence comes this earthly taint?
Surely I love to pray,—but loving it,
    Whence this restraint?

Is there a soul on earth so clogged as mine?
    That mounts on such poor wing?
Surely there is no song of praise so mean
    As that I sing.

Yet it is eager for exultant flight
    And sometimes how it longs
To pour into Thy loving, gracious ear,
    Exultant songs!

Oh blest are they whose conflicts are no more,
    Whose love flows forth to Thee
In a resistless tide that ebbs and flows
    Like a deep sea!

THE POWER OF CHRIST

I.

Oh is it possible that I, a sinner,
  Shall be, one day, a saint?
That life's hard conflict ever shall be over,
  And ended all complaint?

II.

Shall I be cleansed and washed, and then invited
  To be the Master's guest?
Has He a bridal robe for me provided,
  In which I shall be drest?

III.

It cannot be! It seems as if such records
  As stand against my name,
Could not be wiped away, must stand forever
  To be my lasting shame.

IV.

Oh Jesus, make me know what half I'm knowing
  The power of Thy blood,
Plunge Thou this faithless and this sinful creature
  Deep, deep within its flood!

LOVE TO CHRIST

Dear Saviour, if I love Thee not
    I know not what love means;
I live upon Thy smile, I warm,
    I sun me in its beams;
And drinking at Thy fountain sweet
    Care not for other streams.

But do I give a generous love?
    Is it so rich and free,
That I can give no more, dear Lord,
    No more be asked of me?
Is my heart really filled as full
    As human heart can be?

Nay, if it be, yet fill it, Lord,
    With more than it can hold;
Give me that I may give, until
    My loving arms enfold,
Not Thee alone, but Thy whole world
    In myriads untold!

THE BROKEN WING

Have patience and have faith
The surgeon saith,
Suffer awhile this irksomeness of pain;
This broken limb shall soon be well again;
Yea, what is more,
Be stronger for all service than before.

So come I, broken heart,
To ease thy smart,
With promises the future shall make good.
Bear thou in patience Sorrow's solitude,
For she, at length
Will lead thee forth in manliness and strength.

Yes, and in strength unknown
When joy alone
Held thee within her nerveless arms, until
Thou hadst lost courage, lost all force of will.
God will restore
That which He brake, and give it strength the more.

Will make thee strong and wise
To sympathize;
For thou wilt know to soothe, with tender hand,
The sufferings thou hast learned to understand;
And to the weak
What words of inspiration thou wilt speak!

Thou wilt be strong in love;
Soft as a dove,
Yet hovering as on eagle's wings around
The spot where loneliness and grief are found,
And healing bring,
In grateful memory of a broken wing.

Thou wilt have strength unpriced
To work for Christ!
To testify of Him whom pain alone

Could to the human soul Himself make known;
    To watch and pray,
Stronger upon each morrow than today.

GOD IS FOR ME

"When I cry unto Thee then shall mine enemies turn back: this I know: for God is for me."—Psalm 56:9.

Turn back, mine enemy, unmoved
    Thy wiles, thy snares I see;
Turn back, for when I cry to God
    I know He is for me.

Thy day is over; I no more
    Thy willing slave can be,
For I have learned to cry to God;
    I know He is for me.

Hence with thy strong delusions, hence,
    I parley not with thee,
But mid thy temptings cry to God,
    I know He is for me.

Ah, if thou knewest as I know
    The God to whom I flee,
Thou wouldst not think to gain mine ear;
    I know He is for me!

FESTAL DAYS

I.

Thou hast thy festal days, my soul,
  Thou hast had one today!
How gracious was the Master's voice,
  How sweet it was to pray.
In all the world oh can there be,
  A greater joy than thine,
Who hast seen Jesus, and hast felt
  His love upon thee shine?

II.

Yet crave not, ask not, that thy life
  Be fashioned of such days;
Take what God gives, and question not
  The mystery of His ways;
Sit at His table when His voice
  Shall to that table call;
Yet when He bids not, be content
  With crumbs that from it fall.

III.

Oh blessed Jesus! Thou art good
  When I may see Thy face,
And just as good, when though I cry
  Thou wilt not grant that grace.
Giving, I love Thee in Thy gifts,
  Thy gracious Name adore.
Withholding, I will love Thee, Lord,
  And cling to Thee the more!

SPEAK OF CHRIST

I.

Oh speak to me of Christ! No name
    Falls on my ravished ear
With half the music, half the charm,
    That makes it bliss to hear
A loving voice pronounce that word
    As one who holds it dear.

II.

Hast thou not in some favored hour
    Beheld Him face to face,
And canst thou not make known to me
    Its beauty and its grace,
And lure me on to seek for Him
    In some familiar place?

III.

Hast thou not feasted on His word,
    And found it meat indeed,
And canst thou not a fragment spare
    On which my soul may feed,
Some promise, whispered by His lips
    To meet my sorest need?

IV.

Has He not revelations made
    In sacred hours to thee,
That thou canst hold as sacred trust,
    And yet confide to me
Who love, but fain would love Him more,
    Have seen, yet more would see?

V.

Yes, speak of Christ! As one who speaks
    Of his familiar friend,
As one who sees Him every day,
    May on His steps attend,

As one who oft, on reverent knee
Before Him loves to bend.

VI.

Speak with a living warmth, a glow
That shall my heart enflame,
And with thy rich and conscious love
Put my poor love to shame,
Until I, too, have learned to speak
That dearest, dearest Name!

NOT FIT TO GO

I have been forth upon my Master's work
    And yet I know
I was not fit His work to undertake,
    Not fit to go.

I fancied that He sent me, that he said
    "The work is Mine,
But lo I have entrusted it to thee,
    And it is thine."

Alas, I went with banner floating high,
    Strong in my pride;
And bitterly came back, with my whole self
    Dissatisfied.

Dear Lord, art Thou so poor? Couldst Thou not find
    A hand more meet
To bear Thy gifts? See, it is stained and soiled,
    And my tired feet.

Are all adust with wanderings from Thee;
    I blush with shame,
When I go laden with the Bread of Life,
    Or speak Thy name.

Oh cleanse these hands, and from these feet shake off
    The dust of sin;
Rid me of all my curses, make me pure
    Without, within.

For blessed are the hands that wait on Thee,
    And blest the feet
That speed them on Thy missions and that know
    Thy service sweet.

WITH GREAT DELIGHT

"I sat down under His shadow with great delight."
"I will abide under the shadow of the Almighty."

With great delight! Yes, so I sat and rested in His shade,
When of the burden of the day, and of its glare afraid;
I felt myself protected, saved, looked up and saw His face,
How beautiful in tenderness, how wonderful in grace!

With great delight! Life pressed me sore, I knew not where to flee,
In all the world I saw no room, no sphere, no work for me;
He called me to this sheltered spot, rebuking my despair,
I went, and oh the joy I found, the peace I tasted there!

With great delight! A loving friend had fallen at my side,
My eyes were blinded by my tears, my heart within me died;
I staggered from the empty world into this dear retreat,
And found my bitter grief assuaged, yea found my sorrow sweet.

With great delight! My heart is fixed, its endless wants I know,
Forth from this shelter I henceforth will never, never go;
Here in the shadow of God's love forever I'll abide,
So glad, so blest, so sure, so safe; so more than satisfied!

OH COME TO CHRIST

I.

Oh come to Christ! a single glance
   Would melt your doubts away,
One glance would flood you with His light
   And an eternal day.

II.

Oh come to Christ! He waits for you,
   Long has He waiting stood,
Stooping to ask you for your heart,
   Yearning to do you good.

III.

Oh come to Christ! the world has proved
   To thee a broken reed;
Thou canst not trust what always fails
   In time of sorest need.

IV.

Oh come to Christ! for peace, for rest,
   For all thy heart can crave,
For triumph over pain and loss,
   The deathbed and the grave.

THEY HAVE BEEN WITH JESUS

"And they took knowledge of them," etc.

Have they not been with Jesus? See how their faces shine,
With a radiance unearthly, with a glow almost divine,
His mark is on their foreheads, His grace is in their smile,
Every feature is the witness of a spirit without guile.

They must have been with Jesus! for truly they alone,
Who dwell with Him can ever catch the sweetness of his tone,
What tenderness, what earnestness, is breathed in every note,
What thrills of joy melodious within its cadence float.

They have been much with Jesus! no better proof it needs
Than the beauty and the kindliness of all their holy deeds,
Theirs are the hands that minister to want and to distress,
That into every bitter cup a healing cordial press.

They have been long with Jesus! within His blessed school,
They have yielded meek obedience to lesson and to rule,
The wisdom of their teachings mark the graces of their speech,
Which guides the weak and ignorant, yet may the highest reach.

Yes, they have been with Jesus! and counting all things dross,
Have bent, for His dear sake, beneath the burden of His cross;
What chastened, humbled souls are theirs, how unto His akin,
Thrice blessed are ye gracious ones, all heaven is yours to win.

THE FRIEND OF THE LONELY

With Christ ever present, I should not be lonely
    Alone in mid ocean, or desert afar;
I long for Thy presence! I watch for Thy coming,
    Who art Sun of my day, who of night art my Star!

I have known Thee in sorrow, in joy I have known Thee,
    Thou hast wiped away tears, in my gladness been glad;
Thou hast pitied me, cared for me, borne with my follies,
    Been with me when happy, been with me when sad.

Where art Thou now? of the lonely I'm lonely—
    Mid plenty I'm starving, with nothing sufficed;
Friends gather round me, I know them, I love them,
    But oh I am weary, aweary for Christ.

Ah, let me be weary! But let me be patient;
    If Thou hast been mine, Lord, then still Thou art mine;
Weeping through midnight may last, but the morning,
    Sooner or late through the darkness shall shine.

UNDER THE ROD

In vain I seek to hide it from myself,
    My heart is sorrowful, is full of tears;
New grief awakes the echoes of the past,
    I live again through pangs of parted years.

Dear Jesus, it is well! here at Thy feet
    I thank Thee for the past, the present press
Close to my heart of hearts; I love Thy blows,
    Would not evade them, would not wish them less.

How wise, how good Thou art! my wayward will
    Left to itself would lead me all astray,
My wisdom is all ignorance, nor can
    My blinded eyes trace out Thy perfect way.

I want to be like Thee, I want to dwell
    Forever with Thee, and full well I know
Thy path is lowly, full of thorns, yet there
    Where Thou hast been Thy followers must go.

I want a spirit that shall strive and cry
    No more, dear Lord, but meek and humble be,
I want the lowly temper of a child,
    Its weanedness, and its docility.

Thou who hast sent this sorrow, send with it
    A supple will that yields itself to Thine;
That blends itself, is lost in Thy dear will,
    That henceforth shall of nought say, "This is mine!"

Yea, on the pathway of this sorest pain,
    I come to meet Thee, wilt Thou condescend,
To let me find Thee in it, who art more,
    Ten thousand more than dearest earthly friend!

THE WORK OF PEACE

Let me not wait for a new grief to prove me,
    But now while all around me wears a smile,
Dear Jesus, with new love oh let me love Thee,
    With gladder thoughts of Thee the way beguile.

I want to love Thee more, to feel Thee dearer,
    To honor Thee in word and look and tone,
I want to feel Thee ever drawing nearer,
    To be more Thine, and to be less mine own.

Sorrow in times now past has often laid me
    Humble, and empty, down at Thy dear feet,
She only broken-hearted could have made me,
    And taught me to find tribulation sweet.

Shall peace and joy do less for me than sorrow?
    Canst Thou not make them also lay me low?
From them too also may my soul not borrow
    Guidance to Thee? of Thee yet more to know?

Oh lead me on, my Saviour, bide no halting—
    On to the secret spot where Thou dost dwell—
Lead me beyond temptation's rude assaulting—
    Led on by joy or sorrow, all is well!

WHY EMPTY AND SAD?

Other hearts are full, are full of Jesus,
  Why is thine so empty and so sad?
Is it not His work to cheer and please us,
  Is there nothing in Him to make glad?

Say not thou are stript of all thy treasures—
  Rather say the bands that held me fast,
Have been rent in twain that higher pleasures
  My poor, starving soul may seek at last.

Ah, no words there are to tell the sweetness
  Of the soul, that, letting all things go,
Finds itself at rest in Christ's completeness,
  Finds Him solace for its every woe.

Yet the song has rung through all the ages,
  Oft the story sufferers have told;
How He lighted up life's darkest pages,
  Bound, with his own hands, the tale in gold!

Come and try, thou sad and sorrowing spirit,
  What He is in loss, and grief, and pain;
Thou for mourning shall His peace inherit,
  And for sighs take up a joyful strain.

REST

Ah, there is much in this strange life that saddens,
    And much that brings discomfort and unrest,
And there is much that beautifies and gladdens,
    Foretaste of heaven's fullness mid the blest.

Sadness looks downward; sees the shadows lengthen,
    Mid graves of the departed loves to roam;
Gladness looks upward, ebbing faith to strengthen,
    Lives in the promised land and bears right home.

I know them both. I have clasped hands with sorrow,
    And through the ranks of long succeeding years,
Have said I cannot boast me of tomorrow,
    My bread a stony grief, my drink but tears.

And I know joy; the joy that is victorious
    O'er pain and smart, that triumphs in despair,
That looks at suffering and declares it glorious
    To weep with Christ, His fellowship to share.

And now if He should come and freely offer
    To let me make of one of these my choice,
Should I, with grateful heart, accept the proffer,
    And in this freedom of my will rejoice?

Oh no! I want not freedom! Give me rather
    Sense of Thy will, my God, opposed to mine,
I am a little child, and Thou my Father,
    I have no rights, they all are merged in Thine.

Give me or pain or gladness at Thy pleasure,
    Give what Thy wisdom and Thy love may choose,
But be Thou of my soul the hidden treasure,
    And all that soul's defilement let me lose.

For oh, I would be Thine, would walk beside Thee,
    Would know Thee who Thou art, Thy face would see,
My heart is fixed, whatever may betide me,
    It shall have rest, for there is rest in Thee.

CHRIST ON THE SHORE

Lord, blessed be Thy name that Thou dost stand
    Upon life's shore to regulate the flow
Of its wide ocean; that Thy grace has planned
    Its boundaries, doth all its motions know.

For if its tides were ever coming in,
    All would give way before its tumult wild;
We should become the sport of pain and sin,
    Tossed on the raging billows, like a child.

Cheer then, thou tempted soul! though for awhile
    The tempest sweep thee with resistless might,
The tide shall ebb, and thou again shalt smile
    On peaceful waters, sparkling through the night.

And cheer thyself, poor heart! this storm of pain
    That sweeps thee all before it, shall be stayed,
The Son of God will hurl it back again,
    Whose mighty hand hath earth's foundations laid.

Thus far the waves may come, but when they reach
    His chosen limits, thou art safe, art free;
He lets them loose upon thee, but to teach
    How strong, how merciful, His arm can be.

Thou art no thing of chance; His watchful eye
    Notes just how far thou on the shore art thrown;
Bruised, buffeted, bewildered, thou mayst be,
    But dost not suffer friendless and alone.

Cheer thee, faint heart! Beyond the ebb and flow
    Of mortal shores, there shines a crystal sea,
Where thou shalt lie at rest, and cease to know
    Floods of temptation, waves of agony.

There ever dwells on that eternal shore,
    The risen Son of God; to make it thine,
The fearful winds and waves of time He bore,
    Tempted, yet sinless; suffering, yet divine.

Cheer thee, sad heart! In smiling ranks there stand
    Millions of rescued souls, for aye at rest;
Rough waves and billows tossed them to the strand,
    Not rougher are the waves that thou must breast.

AT CHRIST'S TABLE

I go to meet Thee at Thy table, Lord,
    Hear Thou my prayer,
The inmost, deepest longing of my heart,
    And meet me there.

The wedding-garment of Thy righteousness
    Do Thou prepare,
And with the hands that once for me were pierced,
    Enrobe me there.

Reveal to me the burden of the cross
    Thou once didst bear,
Let me too bend beneath it and behold
    And love Thee there.

And when the feast is spread, choose Thou a great
    Or scanty share
For me, as best it pleaseth Thee, and deign
    To feed me there.

Sweet festival! Sweet Lord! Sweet bread and wine!
    I will repair
To it in love and silent gratitude;
    O Christ, be there!

IS THE HEART READY?

Lord, is my heart prepared to meet
    The answer to its prayers,
To stoop at Thy behest, beneath
    The cross that Jesus bears,
To smart beneath the scorn and shame
That they must taste who own His name?

Thou who canst penetrate the folds
    That hide my feeble faith,
Bring forth and try it, heeding not
    What my poor nature saith—
I would be fully known to Thee,
As I would have Thee known to me.

Ah, let my words fall far below
    The fervor of my soul,
Let me not offer Thee a part
    But freely give the whole,
Jesus my Lord, in asking this,
I ask both poverty and bliss.

For he who empty is alone,
    Can by Thy grace be filled,
The thirsty, hungry soul, Thy hand
    Alone to reach is skilled;
And yet how faint that soul must be
Ere it will own its all to Thee!

But when, with hardly strength to cry,
    It casts its languid eye
Upon Thy riches, a new life
    Will through its pulses fly;
Thenceforth how truly it will rest,
An infant on its mother's breast.

"GOD IS HERE"

I.

Within a desert's rough embrace
　A single flower was thrown;
Denied communion with her race
She stood in this wide dwelling-place
　Neglected and alone.

II.

Yet, mid this changeless solitude
　She sighed not to be great,
Secure from pride's impatient mood,
It was her pleasant daily food,
　Her Master's time to wait.

III.

A weary traveler passed that way—
　That weary way, at length,—
With trustless heart and faint, he lay
Upon the sands, to weep away
　His manliness and strength.

IV.

The little stranger flower was nigh—
　Her voice was on his ear,
And faith and joyful trust, sprang high
To weary limb and heart and eye,
　From her brief, *"God is here!"*

V.

Uprose the fainting man, and blessed
　The truth, and blessed the flower;
Companionship and life and rest,
As future paths his footsteps pressed,
　Were his, from that bright hour.

VI.

Oh thou! who livest a useless thing,
Thine errand here much questioning,

"Hope on! hope ever!"
Dwelling from worldly toil apart,
Thy voice through some distrusting heart
  Shall thrill forever.
Wait on, wait on, do not thou fear,
If thou canst only whisper, *"God is here!"*

THE SCHOOL

I.

We are scholars, nothing but scholars,
  Little children at school,
Learning our daily lessons,
  Subject to law and rule.

II.

Life is the school, and the Master
  Is the Man Jesus Christ,
We are His charity scholars,
  His the teaching unpriced.

III.

Slowly we learn, all His patience
  Is hourly put to the test;
But often the slowest and dullest,
  He pities and loves the best.

IV.

Still, we sit at the feet of our Master,
  Very low at His feet.
Study the lessons He sets us,
  Sometimes lessons repeat.

V.

Some of the lessons are pleasant,
  Pleasant, and easy to learn;
The page of our task-book simple,
  Simple and easy to turn.

VI.

But anon the reading is painful,
  Studied mid sighing and tears;
We stammer and falter over it,
  Do not learn it for years.

VII.

Yet that is no fault of the Master;
  All His lessons are good;

Only our childish folly
  Leaves them misunderstood.

VIII.

And still we go on, learning,
  And learning to love our school;
Learning to love our Master,
  Learning to love His rule.

IX.

And by and by, we children
  Shall grow into perfect men,
And the loving, patient Master
  From school will dismiss us then.

X.

No more tedious lessons,
  No more sighing and tears,
But a bound into home immortal,
  And blessed, blessed years!

MY KINDRED

Oh that this heart, with grief so well acquainted
Might be a fountain rich and sweet and full
For all the weary that have fall'n and fainted
In life's parched desert, thirsty, sorrowful!

Come unto me, my kindred! I enfold you
In an embrace to sufferers only known,
Close to this heart I tenderly will hold you,
Suppress no sigh, keep back no tear, no groan.

Yes, weep upon this bosom, that upheaving
With anguish upon anguish, knows full well,
Of grief that had not respite or reprieving,
Of tides that on a shoreless ocean swell.

And can I give you joy and rest and healing?
Can I, a human sufferer at best,
Restore the current calm of peaceful feeling,
And to your weariness give welcome rest?

Nay, but I know Who can! My Lord and Master
Give me brave words with which to speak of Thee,
Oh let my grateful tears flow sweeter, faster,
At the remembrance of Thy sympathy!

Thou Man of Sorrows, teach my lips, that often
Have told the sacred story of my woe,
To speak of Thee till stony griefs I soften,
Till hearts that know Thee not, learn Thee to know.

Till peace takes place of storm and agitation,
Till lying on the current of Thy will,
There shall be glorying in tribulation,
And Christ Himself each empty heart shall fill.

Oh Jesus! Sweet Chastiser! Thanks I render
For aching heart, for pain-contracted brow,
For thus alone I learned how true, how tender,
How beautiful, how beautiful art Thou!

CHRIST ASKS FOR ALL

A jealous lover art Thou, oh my God,
 Asking my all from me;
Is it too much to give? Can I refuse
 This all to Thee?

I cannot trust myself, for while I say,
 All that I have is Thine,
There may be hidden in my inmost heart
 Some thing yet mine.

I may be clinging, though I know it not,
 To some long-cherished joy;
I may be clasping, with a childish heart,
 Some childish toy.

I would not have it thus! I would let go
 Of every outward thing,
That I with empty hands, my dearest Lord,
 To Thee may cling.

Thou art enough to satisfy my heart;
 Long years have taught me this,
Take all, but leave Thyself, I cannot ask
 A greater bliss.

THE UNSEEN SPIRIT

When busy with my household tasks throughout the live-long day
An unseen Spirit walks with me and over me holds sway.

When I walk the city's crowded streets, that Spirit walks with me
Interpreting and putting home each object that I see.

When through the woods I wander lost in wonder and delight
That Spirit still is with me making every thing look bright.

When friends are clustered round me, the Spirit too, is there,
Making loving hearts more loving, and fair faces seem more fair.

He speaks to me in whispers that I alone can hear,
Speaks of God and Christ and heaven, in accents sweet and clear.

He urges me to faithfulness, He quickens me in prayer,
He utters precious promises in moments of despair.

Do I love this unseen Spirit, do I follow His behest,
Do I pray Him to abide with me forever in my breast?

Ah yes! I truly love Him! but for Him my truant heart,
From every holy habit forever would depart.

But for Him I should relapse into worldliness and sin,
Should prove a traitor shameful, and let the Tempter in.

Oh blessed, Holy Spirit! Oh never, never leave
My heart a single moment, lest I Thy love should grieve.

With Thee I can do all things, but if Thou turn away,
I, faithless and ungrateful, should forever go astray!

A PRAYER FOR CHARITY

I.

O Lord, Thou pitiest more than Thou dost blame
  My sin and shame;—
When I, a fallen creature, do condemn
My brother-man, and do his sin contemn,
Thou to the downcast sinner bring'st release,
"Neither do I condemn thee, go in peace."

II.

Oh for a spirit unto Thine akin!
  Oh but to win
A heart of love, a patience like to Thine,
To gain a charity, a love, divine!
In this sad moment when I see my need,
Grant Thou the blessing rare for which I plead.

III.

And when my brother falls, help me to cry
  This might be I;
Thus I, too, should descend without God's grace!
Grant me to look into his downcast face,
With sweet compassion shining upon mine
In heartfelt memory of deeds of Thine!

AT JESUS' FEET

There is a spot where tempted souls
    May find a dear retreat:
They fly from sin and self, and lie
    At Jesus' feet.

In vain upon their heads, the storms
    Of life may rudely beat,
Grief cannot harm the soul that lies
    At Jesus' feet.

My soul, upon life's dizzy heights
    Beware to take thy seat,
Leave not the valley, but abide
    At Jesus' feet.

Would'st thou in peace, and joy and love
    And gladness, stand complete?
Seek it in penitence and faith,
    At Jesus' feet.

A STEADFAST HEART

Keep my heart steadfast, dearest Lord,
　　For earth's allurements shine,
And bid me turn mine eye away
　　From looking into Thine.

Oh keep me steadfast! Earthly tones
　　Fall sweetly on my ear,
And while I pause to list to them
　　Thy voice I cannot hear.

Oh keep me steadfast! Human smiles
　　Delude my childish heart;
While rapt in them how easily
　　From Thee I can depart.

Yes keep me, keep me, for myself
　　I cannot, cannot keep;
Keep me by day, keep me by night
　　O Thou who dost not sleep.

DEATH

I think of Death as of a friend and brother,
    Who, some bright day, will come and call for me,
And lead me to the presence of Another
    With whom I long have pined at home to be.

I know not in what form, or mid what guises
    He will approach me, only this I know,
If he at midnight or at noon surprises,
    I shall clasp hands with him and gladly go.

Have I then nothing that to earth can bind me?
    Has all my oil of gladness been consumed?
Shall not I cast one lingering look behind me,
    Regretting flowers that but for me have bloomed?

Ah, there are few on earth whose human treasures
    More manifold, and costlier are, than mine;
My life is full of joys and full of pleasures,
    Full of the oil of gladness and its wine.

But oh, to go to be with Christ forever!
    To see His face, His wondrous voice to hear!
Never again from Him I love to sever,
    Never to miss His accents on my ear!

So then, my brother, Death, for thee I'm ready;
    I wait, yet woo thee not, abide God's time;
My heart is fixed, my footsteps calm and steady;
    So lead me on to destiny sublime.

Lead me to Christ, lead from all power of sinning,
    Lead me to those who in His image shine;
This will of life be only the beginning,
    And birth, not death, through thee, shall then be mine.

GOD'S SAINTS

God has His saints upon the earth
  Who love Him more than I,
Whose hearts are more attuned to His,
  And yet I know not why.

Who has more reason to fall down
  Before the Father's face,
To thank Him for His sparing love,
  For His redeeming grace?

Whose tears of gratitude should gush
  From fountains full and free,
At memory of more tenderness
  Than Thou hast shown to me?

Lord make me love Thee! Take my heart,
  Establish there Thy throne,
I would be Thine, would have Thee mine,
  O make me all Thine own.

MY EXPECTATION IS FROM THEE

Lord, I have nothing, in myself am nought,
    Weak as a bruised reed Thou findest me;
And yet I dare to call myself Thy child,
    Because my expectation is from Thee.

I am so poor in grace, so weak in faith,
    Seek Thee so feebly on the bended knee;
And yet I must keep seeking, still aspire
    Because my expectation is from Thee.

I long so for Thy presence, yet how oft
    My sins constrain me from Thy face to flee;
I grieve, I falter, but hold on my way
    Because my expectation is from Thee.

I do the deeds I would not, leave undone
    The gracious work that should completed be;
I am ashamed and sorry, yet hope on,
    Because my expectation is from Thee.

And the dread enemy of my poor soul
    Tempts me to yield and fail; but even he
Gives place at mention of Thy dearest name,
    Because my expectation is from Thee.

So self-renouncing, desperate in myself,
    My fallen ruins I can calmly see,
For when I poorest am, all lost and gone,
    My only expectation is from Thee.

WHAT CHRIST CAN BE

Oh that some faithful soul could tell
    What Jesus Christ can be,
To the distracted soul that sinks
    In sorrow's briny sea,
And casts a last despairing look
    To His wide sympathy.

No mother's hand with clasp so soft,
    So true, so kind can press,
And of the gentle, loving tone
    A mother's voice has less;
Yea, she that bare thee is but rough
    To Jesus' tenderness.

Come and behold what Jesus is;
    Into His gracious ear
Pour all the story of thy grief,
    Whisper thine every fear,
And on His sympathizing breast,
    Weep out thine every tear.

Then first the risen Son of God
    Shall unto thee be known,
Then only canst thou feel his heart
    Respond to every groan,
And echo to the bursting sigh,
    The plaintive, helpless moan.

Ah joyful hearts that know not grief
    Can never Jesus know;
He must be learned in darksome nights,
    Where bitter fountains flow,
Where souls are floated off to sea
    By tides of earthly woe.

There have I met Thee, dearest Lord!
    And oh how passing sweet,
Was to my sinking soul, the sound

Of Thine approaching feet—
To point Thee out to drowning ones,
Oh make me, make me meet!

THE SEA OF FIRE

Ah, dearest Master, art Thou really purging
　　My sinful soul within this sea of fire?
To deeper consecration art Thou urging,
　　Plunging me lower but to call me higher?

Small is the pain, not wearisome the bearing
　　The cross Thy hand in mercy lays on me;
Oh let it urge me from the path ensnaring,
　　And lead me nearer, ever nearer Thee.

Pain, in itself, I love not, but its teachings
　　Have been so precious, so have made Thee known,
That my whole soul is making tender reachings,
　　To meet it as it comes, to hear its tone.

Oh come Thou with it! I am very weary
　　Of prosperous days that hide Thy blessed face;
The brightest sunshine makes the landscape dreary,
　　That is not luminous with Thine own grace.

STAYING THERE—COMING BACK

We laid her tenderly away, within her silent bed—
A bed of living flowers of love, trees waving overhead;
With prayers and tears and parting hymn, we left our darling there,
And we came back to life's old work, to miss her everywhere.
We had a single path before, and walked it hand in hand,
But she was weary, stopped to rest, was parted from our band;
We left her lying there alone, a smile upon her face,
And we came back, as tired as she, to see her vacant place;
Left her to sleep in dreamless peace, beneath those guardian trees,
Came back to nights of wakeful grief, and speechless agonies,
Came back to grapple with our hearts, to falter on our way,
To find no language for our grief, no words with which to pray,
Left her in garments that the dust of sin can never soil,
Hers all the joy and all the rest, and ours all the toil.
Farewell, beloved! all is well, we gladly leave thee there,
Come not thou back again to us to join us in life's care;
Our turn will come in God's own time, and we shall sleep with thee,
Where birds can sing, and flowerets bloom, and grass wave peacefully—
Till then thy flesh shall rest in hope, and we will wait the day
When tender hands shall lay us down, to sleep our grief away.

DRAW NEARER!

Draw nearer, O my Saviour, to my soul,
    For Thou art all, and all in all, to me,
Because I feel Thee near I want Thee more,
    Because I love Thee would more loving be.

I am so glad in Thee! A single smile
    A single glance from Thee, can rapture wake,
That finds no words with which to tell its tale,
    And with its joy my heart is like to break.

Draw nearer, nearer yet, reveal Thyself
    To me, Thy child, and oh dear Lord, do Thou
If Thou hast any blessings in reserve,
    Open Thine hand and give those blessings now.

Thou canst give nothing that I do not need,
    For I am very poor, and if I might
Choose for myself, I would not dare to choose,
    I am too ignorant to ask aright.

And when I pray Thee to crowd out of me
    This monster, Self, and then to enter in
And take possession, as a peaceful Guest,
    Do I not ask deliverance from sin?

Do I not ask, within the compass small
    Of these few words, all that there is to give?
Come then, my Saviour, make Thyself a home
    Within this breast, and ever in it live.

Self gone forever, do Thou reign, O Christ,
    The Conq'ror of the conquered, and for aye,
Over each spring of action and of thought,
    Hold Thou within me undisputed sway!

"AND YE ARE CHRIST'S"

"Ye are not your own, bought," etc.
"If the Son therefore shall make you free, ye shall be free indeed."

And we are Christ's! What precious words,
  And oh! the wondrous thought,
That we are not our own but His,
  That He our souls has bought.

Poor slaves to sin and self, how hard
  How wearisome our lot,
We ate the bread of servitude,
  Toiled ever, rested not.

But Christ is Master now, and He
  Has set the captives free,
We weep no more, but sing the song,
  Of perfect liberty.

Yes, we are free to live for Him,
  Free to accept His grace,
To sing His praises, love His name,
  To see His dearest face.

Such is the freedom that our hearts
  Have fondly learned to crave,
The freedom that the Master's hand
  In loving bounty gave.

Yes, we are Christ's, His freedmen we,
  We are both bond and free,
Free by His choice and bond by ours—
  So let us ever be.

WHEREIN TO GLORY

"Let him that glorieth glory in this, that he understandeth and knoweth me."
—JEREMIAH 9:24.

Lord, have I anything of which to boast,
    Of aught to glory,
Who of myself can only sigh, and tell
    The old, sad story?

Ah yes! for Thou hast stooped low down to me,
    Hast kindly sought me,
And who and what Thou art through long, long years
    Hast taught and taught me.

Slowly I learned, for I was dull of brain,
    Cold in affection;
I was a heedless scholar, giddy, childish,
    Without reflection.

Yet now, my Teacher patient, Thee I know,
    Glory in knowing!
Each hour, each day, a grace, a beauty now,
    To me is showing.

Absorbed in this lesson, all about me
    Looks dim and meagre,
To learn it wholly, learn it all by heart,
    How am I eager!

Oh condescend to tell me, then my Master
    The whole dear story,
And Thy rapt listener with grateful joy
    In Thee shall glory!

"IS IT WELL WITH THE CHILD?"

Yes, it is well! For he has gone from me,
From my poor care, my human fallacy,
Straight to the Master's school, the Shepherd's love.
Blessed are they whose training is above!
He will grow up in Heaven, will never know
The conflicts that attend our life below.
He from his earliest consciousness, shall walk
With Christ Himself in glory; he shall talk
With sinless little children, and his ear
No sound discordant, no harsh word shall hear.
Nay, but I have no words with which to tell,
How well it is with him—how well, how well!

"IS IT WELL WITH THEE?"

Yes, it is well! For while with "anguish wild,"
I gave to God who asked him, my child,
He gave to me strong faith, and peace and joy;
Gave me these blessings when he took my boy.
He gave Himself to me; in boundless grace
Within my deepest depths He took His place;
Made heaven look home-like, made my bleeding heart
In all the grief of other hearts take part;
Brought down my pride, burnt up my hidden dross,
Made me fling down the world and clasp the cross;
Ah how my inmost soul doth in me swell,
When I declare that all with me is well!

GO AND TELL JESUS

Oh aching heart, oh restless brain,
Go and tell Jesus of thy pain;
He knows thee, loves thee, and His eye
Beams with divinest sympathy.

Go and tell Jesus; human ear
Thy mournful story may not hear;
Keep nothing back, for thee He cares,
His patient heart thy burden bears.

Go and tell Jesus; well He knows
The human heart; its pangs, its throes;
He will not fail Thee, He will be
Friend, Comforter, and Peace to thee.

Go and tell Jesus; never yet,
Did He a breaking heart forget;
Press closely to His bleeding side,
There, there thou shalt be satisfied.

A WISH

Oh that with ready grace my heart could give
    What God requires;
That there within it lived no grasping will
    No fond desires.

It grieves, it pains me that I do not fly
    O Christ, to Thee,
To lay this treasure at Thy feet, with sweet
    Alacrity.

Yet take it from me; if I love it much,
    I love Thee more,—
But pity, as Thou takest, for it leaves
    My heart so sore!

HEALING

Low in the dust of self-abasement lying,
O'er a poor, wasted life my heart is sighing,
    Lord Jesus, heal my soul!

I have sought riches, glory, comfort, pleasure;
In Thee I saw no beauty, sought no treasure;
    Lord Jesus, heal my soul!

On husks the swine do eat I have been feeding,
I have resisted all Thy tender pleading;
    Lord Jesus, heal my soul!

How sorrowful, how spent I am, how weary,
Oh in this desert place so dark and dreary,
    Lord Jesus, heal my soul!

WEARINESS

Ah, is there, anywhere, a sorer heart,
    Than this sore heart of mine?
Jesus, have mercy on me, let me lay
    Its griefs on Thine.

If Thou dost fail me, everything will fail;
    Pain be too hard to bear;
Then dost Thou pity me that I am sad?
    Lord, dost Thou care?

All eyes, save mine, may weep, but not for me
    Is the refreshing tear;
My tears are prayers, are speechless sighs and groans;
    O, dost Thou hear?

THE ORANGE-TREE

Be like the faithful plant that not content
    With bearing fruitage as a yearly store,
While that fruit ripens, blossoms out anew,
    That they who plucked may come and pluck once more.

Let those who seek thee find that blossoms rare
    Deck thy meek bosom as with bridal grace,
Sweet charity adorn thee, tender smiles
    Light up and render beautiful thy face.

And then surprise them with a harvest full
    Of glorious deeds, who fancied they should find
Fragrance and loveliness, but did not dream
    To gather also food for heart and mind.

EVER AT WORK

Ever at work, my weary hands
    Might never folded be;
New tasks were ever given, and
    There was no rest for me.

Others sat quietly at ease
    From toilsome labor free;
I ceased not, for the Master said
    There was no rest for me.

The busy world lay down at night
    And slept right peacefully;
I could not sleep, upon my bed
    There was no rest for me.

I faltered, fainted at my task,
    Performed it wearily—
I had no future, lost all hope;
    There was no rest for me.

At last, accustomed to the yoke,
    Rest ceased to be my plea,
I grew familiar with the thought
    That it was not for me.

But when the fabric fair on which
    I worked unceasingly,
Was finished, lo, the Master cried,
    "Now rest within, with Me."

Ah faithless, peevish, childish heart!
    The end thou couldst not see;
The Master Builder did but plan
    A nobler rest for thee!

BACKSLIDING

I.

All I am suffering now is just the portion
  Brought on myself by falling back from Thee
My dearest Friend, in folly most astounding;
  Oh can I pardoned, rescued can I be?

II.

Canst Thou permit me to fall down before Thee,
  Wilt Thou contrition give, and wilt Thou show
Once more Thy face till I again adore Thee,
  Once more Thy voice may hear, Thy grace may know?

III.

Lord Jesus, if Thou dost, I cannot promise
  Henceforth to serve and love but Thee alone;
I cannot trust myself, I am unfaithful;
  Have often wandered, am to wander prone.

IV.

I only come to Thee in desperation;
  Sick of myself, and every word and deed;
Plead Thou my cause, Thou friend of fallen sinners,
  For me Thy erring, sorrowing creature plead.

And oh this wandering heart make strong and steadfast,
  Fix Thou this will that I may rove no more;
Let me see Thee, who art of love an ocean,
  Nor cast one lingering look towards earth's shore.

SO BE IT

So be it; 'tis Thy plan not mine,
  And being Thine is good;
My God, my will shall yield to Thine
  Ere it is understood.

So be it; I a child of dust
  Will not oppose Thy way,
Move on, mysterious Will, I trust,
  I love, and will obey.

So be it; and do Thou, my heart,
  No childish questions ask,
Thou in God's counsels hast no part,
  Crave not so hard a task.

So be it; yes, so be it, Lord,
  No word have I to say—
O be Thy gracious Name adored—
  I love and will obey.

"NEARER TO THEE"

I am alone; no human eye
    Heeds where I am or what I do—
How shall I spend the time, what work
    What pastime shall I now pursue?

If Thou, dear Jesus, wert on earth
    In human form, how soon my feet
Should run to seek Thee; how my heart
    Would listen to Thy counsels sweet.

This leisure hour would soon slip by,
    If in it I might speak to Thee,
If I might tell Thee of my love,
    And know that Thou wert near to me.

But since Thou art not here on earth
    In human form, yet still draw nigh
By Thy blest Spirit, let me feel
    The Son of David passes by.

Give me some token that Thou still
    Canst look from heavenly heights above
With the same pitying tenderness,
    Which once filled earth with sacred love.

I long to feel Thee near, to know
    That I a sinner, yet am Thine,
And what is more, beyond a doubt,
    To know that Thou art truly mine.

To know and feel Thee just as near
    As they who once embraced Thy feet,
Who oft beheld Thy sacred form,
    At pleasure could their Master greet.

Ah nothing less can satisfy
    The heart that hungers so for Thee,
But waking in Thy likeness, Lord,
    From sin and sense forever free.

NIGHT

Dear Lord, I do remember Thou hast said
  That I may cast my every care on Thee;
But see, this deep oppression will not go,
  But with its leaden hands holds fast to me.

Holds fast, and drags me down, and shuts my mouth,
  Strangles the cry that fain would pierce the skies;
Helpless I lie before Thee, with no words
  Upon my lips, with sad yet tearless eyes.

So be it, Lord; my joyous soul has need
  Of its dark days, and in this dreary night;
Roots shall strike downward, that anon shall shoot
  In rich and living branches to the light.

Oh may these branches bear some fruit for Thee,
  In grateful memory of the loving hand,
That cast me in this gloomy, cheerless spot,
  And all its dreariness and darkness planned.

REST

Rest, weary feet!
Rest from your ceaseless wanderings, your travels to and fro,
The countless steps you had to take, fatigue to undergo,
There are no painful paths to tread, here is your journey's end,
The quiet grave shall welcome you and be to you a friend.

Rest, busy hands!
Rest from the labors that you wrought from dawn to set of sun,
From work that only ended when another was begun;
Fold them in peace and leisure now, they have no more to do—
Let the poor tired servants rest, they have been true to you.

Rest, beating heart!
Rest from thy joys tumultuous, from sorrow and from pain,
It shall not faint by joy consumed, it shall not mourn again,
Let it lie down and rest awhile, secure from all alarm,
This grave knows how to quiet it, knows how to bring it balm.

Rest, toiling brain.
Rest from the vigil that consumed, the nights of sleepless care,
From thoughts that tortured and condemned, from tasks it could
    not bear;
Upon this pillow, icy cold, within this narrow bed,
There lies no fevered, wakeful mind, not any aching head.

Rest, eager soul!
Thou hadst thy wings and tried them oft, they fluttered back to earth,
Thy pinions, not like thee, divine, knew not thy heavenly birth;
This grave is not thy home and end, mount upward and away—
Activity shall be thy rest from henceforth and for aye,
Thou shalt find blissful fellowship with souls to thine akin,
Eternal gates shall open wide to let the long-sought in;
Thrice blessed art thou, living soul! Spring homeward to thy rest,
Among the throngs that rest no more, and are forever blest!

FAINT NOT

Faint not beneath the loving Hand
   That wisely chastens thee,
Jesus will make thee understand
   Why this sharp stroke must be.

And if thy pains are long drawn out,
   Oh weary not, be strong,
Suffer in patience, Jesus' love
   Can do thy soul no wrong.

Honor the pangs that come from Him;
   Give thanks for pain and smart,
Thy groans and sighs have echoes found
   Within His sacred Heart.

Oh lonely Sufferer! Oh Lord,
   What agonies were Thine!
Give us, Thy followers, fellowship
   In sorrows so divine.

From thine own bitter cup, let all
   Thy faithful children drink,
Start we not back like coward souls,
   Nor from Thy chastening shrink.

We love Thee, choose Thee, give to us
   What first was given to Thee;
So shall we in Thy likeness grow,
   And one in heart with Thee.

NOT POOR

Call me not poor; I nothing lack,
    For lo, a voice divine
Has made me feel that I am His
    And told me He is mine.

Weep not that on this weary bed,
    I long must droop and pine;
Here I have learned the peace of God,
    And know that He is mine.

Nor mourn that He has torn away
    My idols from their shrine;
Blest be the Hand that gave, that took,
    For Jesus still is mine.

Let heaven's own radiance through the storm
    Of every sorrow shine,
I heave no sigh, I shed no tear,
    Am His, and He is mine.

IN GRIEF AND SHAME

I lie before Thee, Lord, just where I ought
  In grief and shame to lie;
I am not worthy of a glance from Thee;
  Yet do not pass me by.

I have forsaken Thee, an earthly spring
  Yet once again to try;
It leaves me thirsty, may I come to Thee?
  O do not pass me by.

In a sad hour, a false, yet glittering prize,
  Caught and enticed my eye;
I sought, and lost it, in my grief and pain,
  Lord, do not pass me by.

I am so sorrowful, so sick and faint;
  Long so to feel Thee nigh;
Have pity on me, tempted Son of God,
  And do not pass me by.

"IN REMEMBRANCE OF ME"

Dear Jesus, Thou this feast hast spread,
　　Invited guests are we;
We come as Thou hast bid us come,
　　Thus to remember Thee.

We come from sinful thought and aim,
　　More earnestly to flee;
Pardon to seek and grace to find,
　　As we remember Thee.

We come to thank Thee for Thy love
　　So rich, so full, so free;
To bless Thee, praise Thee, lose ourselves,
　　As we remember Thee.

We come to lay the burdens down
　　That press most heavily;
To enter into perfect peace
　　As we remember Thee.

Our penitence, our love, our hope,
　　Oh condescend to see,
And let us "bear a song away"
　　As we remember Thee.

"HE MUST INCREASE, BUT I MUST DECREASE"

A free translation from Lavater.[1]

Oh Jesus Christ, dwell Thou in me,
  And bid all else to vanish;
Bring my heart daily nearer Thee,
  Its sinfulness to banish.

Hover each day, in grace and might,
  Above my weak presuming,
Thy radiance swallowing up my night,
  Thy life my death consuming.

Let Thy pure sun-light on me shine,
  My soul from error freeing;
Thine all, O Christ, and nothing mine,
  My soul Thee only seeing.

Draw near, I cast myself away,
  Weeping, on Thee I'm waiting,
Oh, let Thy holy will have sway,
  Thy will in mine creating.

Look gloriously forth from me,
  In wisdom, grace and gladness;
Let me Thy living image be,
  In happiness and sadness.

Make all within me new, that so
  No human weakness knowing,
Thine own devoted, loving glow
  May in my heart be glowing.

Let pride retreat, and weakness flee,
  And folly find an ending,
When towards Thy kingdom and towards Thee
  My earnest soul is tending.

And may this vain and empty I
  Be every day decreasing;

---

1 Johann Kaspar Lavater (1741–1801) Swiss poet.

And every day that passes by
Behold my faith increasing.

Empty self out of me each day;
Fill with Thy presence dearer,
O Thou who over prayer hast sway,
Be of my prayer the Hearer!

May faith in Thee my impulse prove,
My inmost soul inspire;
Be Thou, O Christ, my joy, my love,
My passionate desire!

NEARER TO CHRIST

I never pressed so close to Thee, my Saviour,
  But inward voices cried, Draw nearer still!
Is my heart then so large, and cannot Jesus
  With His own fulness its deep ocean fill!

What means this aching void? Is there no limit
  To the deep longing of the human soul?
Shall it know hunger and know thirst forever—
  Grasp but in fragments, never seize the whole!

Ah, childish questions! Listen to the answer;
  Great is thy heart, thy soul insatiate;
Yet has not room for Him who rules all nations,
  The coming of whose Kingdom worlds await.

Ask for a larger heart, for longings deeper;
  For richer faith with which to meet this Guest,
Who, wheresoever He finds room, will enter,
  And satisfy the restless with His rest.

WALKING WITH GOD

I.
He walks with God! Enough for me
That this I in my brother see;
I ask not what his rank, or name,
Whether obscure, or rich in fame,
Who fall before him, or who rise;
If he be ignorant or wise.

II.
He walks with God! To Him allied,
He presses closely to His side;
No more of him I ask to know,
But gladly I with him will go;
My brother he, my dearest friend;
With him I would a life-time spend.

III.
He walks with God! Oh, kinship sweet,
For saints and angels only, meet,
How steadfast and how true the heart
That from its Master will not part!
Though never warm or true to me,
I love it, Lord, for loving Thee!

IV.
He walks with God! Nor ever heeds
Over what heights his pathway leads.
Or where to valley dips the road;
Enough for him to be with God;
Enough that earthly joy or pain
Tempting, can only tempt in vain.

V.
He walks with God! I lift mine eye
And see what fields before him lie;
The river clear, the pasture green;
What matters what may intervene?
Lord, when he is at home, with Thee
O let his mantle fall on me!

A CUP OF WATER

Dear Jesus, where wert Thou when I refused
    To give a cup of water for Thy sake?
Where did I part with Thee, how did I dare
    A single step in my own strength to take?

This shows me what I am; it shows that deep
    In my heart's core the love of self still lies;
I have no goodness, in my own conceit
    Oh let me never, never more be wise!

And wilt Thou condescend the cup to fill
    My sinful hands put by, and may the lip
I would not moisten, taste Thy living draught,
    And evermore its strength and sweetness sip!

ANGELS' FOOD

Thou canst eat angels' food, my soul, turn from earth's husks away,
They are not fitted for thy wants, thy hunger cannot stay;
The servants in thy Father's house have better bread than thine
Who art His own adopted one, why then mid plenty pine?

Thou canst of living waters drink, why turn to earthly springs
That at the fountain-head are dry, amid inferior things;
Come to the crystal rivers pure that flow through pastures green,
That make their gladsome sparkling way, the smitten rocks between.

Thou canst inhale, thou pilgrim soul, the atmosphere of heaven,
By Him who deals in bounteous gifts its fullness shall be given,
Then wilt thou in the mortal strife, in human weakness, dare
To breathe amid the vapors foul of earth's sin-tainted air?

Ah foolish soul! ah childish soul! Ah soul on ruin bent,
This world is not thy home, thy rest, thou art in banishment;
Build not with too much care thy nest; thou shalt be stripped and peeled,
Made hungry, thirsty, sick and faint, ere thy disease is healed.

Yet fear thou not and falter not, despise not thou the way;
The long, dark night shall usher in joy's own resplendent day;
Soon safe within thy Father's house by Him thou shalt be fed,
Shalt drink His wine, sit at His feast, and taste the living bread.

What matters then the rage of thirst, the gnaw of hunger's pang,
The cry for air that from thy heart in stifling terror rang?
What matter that thou hast not where on earth to build a nest?
The day is brighter after night, toil only sweetens rest.

TESTIMONY

How gladly would Thy children, Lord,
　In goodly company,
Unite to sound Thy praises out,
　And testify of Thee.

If we oft times in silence sit,
　Thou who our hearts dost know,
Seest a love that finds no words
　And tears that do not flow.

There rests upon our mortal tongues,
　Sometimes a secret spell,
It is not coldness that is mute,
　But love that loves too well.

We thank, we bless Thee, that to Thee
　This is no sinful mood,
That by the depths that dwell in Thine
　Our hearts are understood.

Search us and try us, not alone
　Our sinfulness to see,
But to detect the love that longs
　To testify of Thee.

"AT EVENING TIME THERE SHALL BE LIGHT"

At evening time there shall be light!
    Yes, when the night draws nigh,
When shadows lengthen, and the sun
    Is parting from the sky;
When the warm air grows chill, and earth
    Lies in obscurity;

There shall be light! A light unseen
    Amid the glare of day,
It shall illume the lonely path
    Through which thy footsteps stray,
To guide thee, lure thee, cheer thee on
    Amid the darkest way.

There shall be light! As tender hands
    Light children to their bed,
So shalt thou just as lovingly,
    As tenderly be led,
And shown upon what pillow, thou
    Mayst lay thy weary head.

There shall be light! Yet faith's bright eye
    Alone that light can see;
Can take from death its chill, its gloom,
    And lend it ecstacy;
Look up! And see the risen Christ
    Shine, like the sun, for Thee!

A COLD HEART

I know that I love Thee my Saviour,
Yet my heart lies as cold as a stone,
I have not the strength to grow warmer,
Nor life enough for Thee to groan.

I know that I love Thee, my Saviour,
Yet veiled and unsought is Thy face,
I see not, I hear not, I feel not
Of what I once knew of Thy grace.

I know that I love Thee, my Saviour,
Though withered and stupid and dead,
Though the shower of blessing is failing
And all that has cheered me has fled.

I know that I love Thee, my Saviour!
Away then with fear and with doubt,
Let me rest in this sorrowful prison,
Till Thou Thyself callest me out.

SATISFIED

"I shall be satisfied when I awake with Thy likeness."

What shall I find in heaven? The faces dear
Upon whose love and smiles I feasted here?
Shall I rejoice that naught can there divide
United hearts, and so be satisfied?

What shall I do in heaven? Shall I be blest
With a long luxury and endless rest?
Conflict and labor over, shall I ride
Through seas untroubled, and be satisfied?

What shall I be in heaven? A messenger
Passing from sainted ones to those who err
And suffer still on earth? Mid fields so wide,
Shall I, who love to work, be satisfied?

I know not, care not; when life's fetters break,
When from death's blessed restful sleep I wake,
Whate'er Thy love withhold, or may provide,
Being like Thee, I shall be satisfied!

"MY GOLDEN HOURS"

My golden hours! My golden hours!
  O what and whence, are they?
Have they sprung up mid life's fair flowers,
  Fruits of a sun-lit day?

Have I sailed forth on prosperous seas,
  Bound for the blessed land
Where I could take them at my ease,
  From off a sparkling strand?

Not so! They grew mid brambles rude,
  Sprang up mid briar and thorn,
Mid darkest nights, in solitude,
  My golden hours were born.

On stormy seas the bark was lost
  That sought these treasures rare;
I found them on a rock-bound coast;
  I plucked them from despair.

Now God be praised, who briar and thorn
  Strewed thickly on my way;
My pierced soul, all rent and torn,
  Shall anthems sing for aye.

And blessed be His name, who walked
  Upon life's troubled sea;
Whispered of His own peace, and talked
  As a dear Friend to me.

For in my griefs and pains and sighs,
  Mid chilling frosts and showers,
I won from my dear Lord the prize;
  His golden, golden hours!

THE GIFT

I.

I asked of Thee a gift, Jesus, my Lord,
    And my expectant eyes looked up, to see
That blessing speedily from Thy dear Hand
    Come down to me.

II.

I waited, but it came not; asked again,
    And thought to see it come in angel-guise,
And when it lingered, found no words to tell
    My sad surprise.

III.

Dear Saviour, have I asked amiss, I cried,
    What was there lacking in my earnest prayer;
Did it seek heaven upon too weak a faith
    To enter there?

IV.

Full long I pondered, hoping that the gift
    For which I earnestly my Lord besought,
Would, if attained, fill my whole soul with love,
    And holy thought.

V.

But as He still denied it, did not choose
    To give it me, I cast and threw my will
Down at His feet, and bid it there to lie,
    Patient and still.

VI.

Should not the Hand so bountiful to me,
    Reserve the right to choose for me my good,
Should I not glory in His ways, if they
    Were understood?

VII.

Thus musing, to my closet yet once more
    I stole, if only lovingly to say,

Do what Thou wilt, dear Lord, for Thy "sweet will,"
  Is mine, alway.

VIII.

When lo, within that closet, waiting me,
  I found the risen Christ, and oh what grace,
What love, what beauty and what tenderness,
  Shone in His face!

IX.

And thus He spake, "That was but seeming good,
  Thy childish ignorance so boldly craved,
Withholding it My love protected thee,
  From danger saved.

X.

"But I have come instead; yes, here am I,
  Thy longed-for Saviour; lean upon my breast,
Thy disappointment shall give place to joy,
  To peace and rest!"

XI.

Ah Lord! too sacred was that wondrous hour!
  The veil that hides it let no mortal lift;
Great was the grace I sought, but oh how small
  Beside Thy gift!

JOINT HEIR WITH CHRIST

"It is enough for the disciple that he be as his Lord."

I.

What aileth thee, my heart? Thy lamentations
    Fill all the air, yet Jesus draweth nigh;
This is His gift, the sorrow thou deplorest;
    He chose this anguish, counted out each sigh;
    The Son of David would not pass thee by.

II.

Wounded, imprisoned heart, He comes for healing,
    From thy captivity to set thee free,
Thy blinded eyes He comes Himself to open,
    The sore, sad weight to render sweet to thee;
    He passes by, and thou His face canst see.

III.

Thou falterest, my heart? Then lay thy burden
    At His dear feet, who came the cross to bear:
Give Him this grief; upon the Man of sorrows
    Lay thou thy sorrows, lay thine every care,
    And overwhelm Him with thy deep despair.

IV.

For as his Lord shall not be the disciple;
    Christ may endure the cross and bear the shame;
He may walk homeless, sleep without a pillow,
    And He who for our sakes a Man became,
    Have scorn and anger heaped upon His name.

V.

But thou, self-lover, choosest ease and leisure,
    Thou with this Man of sorrows hast no part;
Thou must have home and friends and reputation,
    A life of peace, an unencumbered heart,
    Pleasure's bright sparkle, not affliction's smart!

VI.

For shame! For shame! Arise in strength courageous,
    Bear thine own burden though it be with tears;

Follow the Master, imitate His patience,
   If need be, follow three and thirty years,
   Mid poverty, mid loneliness and fears.

VII.

It is enough that of His grief partaker,
   Thou shalt with Him in all His glory share;
Shalt own the love that meted out thy sorrows,
   Proclaim His praise, His faithfulness declare,
   And with Him enter heaven His joint heir!

GOD'S WAY

Dear Lord, I often tell Thee that I fain
    Would give some great and costly gift to Thee;
Yea, I have almost courted loss and pain,
    If I thereby might proved and humbled be.

And now the Hand that I have asked to take
    From out my store some dear, some precious thing,
Does not disdain this bruised heart to break,
    To get possession of its offering.

Yes, blood-drops ooze from many a rent that Thou
    Thyself hast torn, and I am faint and sore;
I feel a death-like moisture on my brow
    And on my dizzy brain wild voices roar.

But oh I waver not! Thou knowest well
    I meant that Thou shouldst take me at my word,
The bitter waves of anguish rise and swell,
    But heed them not, my Master and my Lord.

Keep what Thou hast in wise and tender grace,
    Snatched from my deepest depths, nor left to me
Option or choice; love shines upon Thy face,
    Thou knowest best what I can spare for Thee.

But oh, by all this pain, this bleeding heart,
    Subdue, control, beat down and lay me low;
New knowledge of Thyself to me impart,
    Jesus, my Saviour, let me learn to know.

I smart, I writhe, I bleed—and still I cry—
    Lo that Thou hast is Thine, is mine no more;
Thou Master of my treasures art, and I
    In this new poverty Thy name adore!

PRAYER

My soul is weak, its purposes are poor,
Of nothing in itself it can be sure,
Nor knows that to the end it can endure;
    And so I love to pray.

My heart is cold, it does not always beat
With glowing love to Jesus, as is meet,
Nor always run His blessed form to greet;
    And so I love to pray.

My mind is ignorant and dark; I know
So little of the way in which to go,
My progress is so tedious and so slow,
    And so I love to pray.

For praying, I can feel that God is strong,
That in my weakness I to Him belong,
That He can nothing do or false or wrong—
    Dearly I love to pray!

And my cold heart grows warmer as it tells
Its story pitiful, with love it swells
To Him who unseen ever near it dwells,
    And so I love to pray.

And in communing with the great All-Wise,
What scales drop off from my poor, blinded eyes!
What gracious lessons He to me supplies!
    Ah Lord! I love to pray!

WHERE IS HE?

Oh where is He for whom my soul is pining,
    For whom I yearn, and thirst, and pant, and pray?
Around His empty cross my arms I'm twining,
    What daring hand has borne His form away?

He is my soul's beloved, my heart's treasure—
    With Him this weary world could restful be;
Without Him language is too poor to measure,
    How desolate, how homeless it would be.

Say you the Lord has left His cross behind Him
    For you to hang on, and from hence is gone?
Gone? Whither? But my heart shall go and find Him,
    Nor linger here, defrauded and forlorn.

Tell me, how went He? Point in the direction
    And I will follow wheresoe'er He leads;
All paths are one to passionate affection—
    That neither time, nor pain, nor peril heeds.

What say you? He has homeward gone, and left me
    To follow thither? Gladly, Lord, I come!
I knew Thou hadst not of Thyself bereft me—
    One moment more and I too am at home!

What hands invisible are these that hold me,
    And beat me back, and will not let me go?
Cease to oppose, presume not to enfold me—
    I fly to Him I love, to Him I know.

I may not, say ye? May not hope to clasp Him
    Save in the ministry of pain and loss,
My loving arms may never reach to grasp Him
    Save through His martyrdom and on His cross!

Quick with the nails then! Spare not for my crying
    Where my Beloved hung let me too hang—
In this sweet agony death is not dying—
    The pang that bears to Him, it is no pang!

THE MOTHER

I.

As I have seen a mother bend
  With aching, bleeding heart,
O'er lifeless limbs and lifeless face—
  So have I had to part

II.

With the sweet prattler at my knee,
  The baby from my breast,
And on the lips so cold in death,
  Such farewell kisses prest.

III.

If I should live a thousand years
  Time's hand cannot efface,
The features painted on my heart
  Of each beloved face.

IV.

If I should bathe in endless seas
  They could not wash away
The memory of these children's forms;—
  How fresh it is today.

V.

Ah, how my grief has taught my heart
  To feel another's woe!
With what a sympathetic pang
  I watch the tear-drops flow!

VI.

Dear Jesus! must Thou take our lambs,
  Our cherished lambs away?
Thou hast so many, we so few—
  Canst Thou not let them stay?

VII.

Must the round limbs we love so well,
  Grow stiff and cold in death?
Must all our loveliest flowerets fall
  Before his icy breath?

VIII.

Nay Lord, but it is hard, is hard—
 Oh give us faith to see,
That grief, not joy, is best for us
 Since it is sent by Thee.

IX.

And oh, by all our mortal pangs
 Hear Thou the mother's plea—
Be gracious to the darling ones
 We've given back to Thee.

X.

Let them not miss the mother's love,
 The mother's fond caress;
Gather them to Thy gentle breast
 In faithful tenderness.

XI.

Oh lead them into pastures green,
 And unto living springs;
Gather them in Thine arms, and shield
 Beneath Thy blessed wings.

XII.

Ah, little reck we that we weep,
 And wring our empty hands;—
Blessed, thrice blessed are infant feet,
 That walk Immanuel's lands!

XIII.

Blessed the souls that ne'er shall know
 Of sin the mortal taint,
The hearts that ne'er shall swell with grief
 Or utter a complaint!

XIV.

Brief pangs for us, long joy for them!
 Thy holy Name we bless,
We could not give them up to Thee,
 Lord, if we loved them less!

"OH COME THOU DOWN TO ME, OR TAKE ME UP TO THEE!"

I would be with Thee, dearest Lord, I long Thy face to see,
I long that each succeeding day should bring me nearer Thee;
Wilt Thou come down to dwell with me, wilt Thou with me abide;
Wilt Thou go with me where I go, be ever at my side?

Thy home is with the humble, Lord; that blessed truth I know;
But cannot change my heart myself, do Thou, then, make it so;
Oh come, my Saviour, come to me, it is not life to live,
Unless thy presence fills my soul, except Thyself Thou give.

Or, if Thou canst not come to me, a weak, a sinful child,
If Thou, alas, dost find in me no temple undefiled,
Oh then my gracious Lord, send down a messenger for me,
And strip my sinfulness away and take me up to Thee.

I care not where I find Thee, Lord, whether or here or there,
I only know I want to find and love Thee, everywhere;
This world with all its tears and groans, would be my chosen place,
If Thou shouldst plan it for the scene in which to show Thy face.

And heaven with all its peace and rest, would be no heaven to me,
If I might dwell forever there, without a glimpse of Thee;
It is not life, or life's best joys, it is not heaven I want,
But oh, Thou risen Christ, for Thee, for Thee alone, I pant!

"DYING, YET BEHOLD WE LIVE"

A ship, full laden left her native port,
    To plough the waves, and seek another clime;
Her sails were set, and gallant ranks of men,
    If the wind failed, would with their oars keep time.

Her port she left, but on a troubled main,
    Her every sinew, every nerve, she strained;
Yet wooed the breezes, spread her sails in vain—
    She sped not on her way, nor land she gained.

Then rose the pilot, "Heed my words," he cried;
    "Too many a weighty gift this ship ye gave;
Cast this and that away, and she shall ride
    Lightly, and unencumbered, o'er the wave."

With niggard hand, reluctantly they drew
    Some trifles from her breast, and in the sea
They one by one these secret treasures threw,
    And saw them sink in its immensity.

Yet still, as if held back by leaden hands,
    The ship no progress made, and so once more,
The pilot, working her from off the sands,
    Made the same plaint his voice had made before.

Then one by one her treasures left her deck,
    To be by yawning, briny jaws consumed,
And mid fierce winds and storms, an empty wreck,
    Went staggering into port, condemned and doomed.

And yet the pilot from the master won
    Plaudits and welcomes that his zeal repaid,
For on his ear there fell the glad well done,
    Who, faithful to his trust, no trust betrayed.

Thus, O my soul, thy Pilot made thy way
    Straight to the haven where thou fain wouldst be;
Nor feared to rob thee, cut thy spars away,
    Knowing the Master only cared for thee.

For thee, dismantled, empty, good for naught,
For thee, who unto him no treasure bore;
Then ride at anchor, tempest-tossed, distraught,
For thou hast touched at an eternal shore!

ONLY JESUS

From the German.[1]

Jesus, Jesus, only Jesus,
    Shall become my wish and aim;
Now I make a sacred promise
    That our wills shall be the same;
For my heart in sweet accord,
Cries, "Thy will be done," dear Lord!

There is One whom I am loving,
    Loving early, loving late;
He to me my all has given,
    All to Him I consecrate,
Thou Thy blood on me hast poured,
Let Thy will be done, dear Lord!

If what seems to be a blessing
    Is not chosen, planned by Thee,
Oh deprive me of it, rather
    Give me what is good for me;
Still Thy name shall be adored,
Where Thy will despoils me, Lord!

Let Thy will be done within me,
    Through me, by me, ever done,
Done in life, in joy, in sorrow,
    Till the victory is won.
Dying, be in me restored,
When, how, where Thou wilt, dear Lord!

---

1 Ludämilia Elisabeth (1640–1672) German poet.

"YOUR DARLING SLEEPS"

A very free translation from the German.[1]

I.

Your darling sleeps; bid not his slumbers cease,
 Permit this sweet repose;
Lying among the flowers, and full of peace,
 He says, to soothe your woes—
I lie enfolded in delightful rest,
The lines have fall'n to me among the blest—
 Your darling sleeps.

II.

Your darling sleeps; all wearied out with play
 And satisfied with joy;
Forgotten now is what beguiled the day,
 Forgotten festival, and book, and toy,
The treasures that he loved can charm no more,
For his young feet have climbed to Eden's door—
 Your darling sleeps.

III.

Your darling sleeps; his day of life was gay
 And rich in joyous hours;
A sparkling brook that made its gladsome way
 Through fields of blooming flowers;
Sorrow nor knew him or his presence sought,
With him not death itself in conflict wrought—
 Your darling sleeps.

IV.

Your darling sleeps; how blessed and how sure,
 On the good Shepherd's arm!
His childish heart from sinful stain made pure,
 Death could not do him harm;
Compassed with holy nurture, holy care,
His dying pillow was parental prayer—
 Your darling sleeps.

---

1 Paul Gerok, German poet.

V.

Your darling sleeps; and so he sleeps away
    Life's bitter, threatening hours;
Know'st thou, oh mother, what concealed lay,
    Amid its adverse powers?
Now wintry storms for him may vainly beat,
Vainly may summer scorch with fervid heat,
    Your darling sleeps.

VI.

Your darling sleeps; but for a single night,
    Whose gloomy shades must flee;
And when the day dawns forth with rosy light.
    That will a morning be!
The Man of sorrows, pitying your grief,
Will come, as once of old, to your relief—
    Your darling sleeps.

VII.

Your darling sleeps; and now the parting kiss
    Upon his white lips press;
O mother-heart, through such an hour as this
    Christ pity your distress!
He walks upon life's billows, and He will
Allay the storm and all its moanings still—
    Your darling sleeps.

VIII.

Your darling sleeps; close to Thy tender breast,
    Good Shepherd, clasp our trust!
Ye stars, look kindly on his place of rest,
    And guard his precious dust!
Ye winds float round him on a gentle wing,
Ye flowers, a lavish fragrance o'er him fling!
    Our darling sleeps.

NEARER

Oh Jesus, draw nearer,
And make Thyself dearer,
I yearn, I am yearning for Thee;
Come take for Thy dwelling,
The heart that is swelling
With longings Thy beauty to see!

How languid and weary,
How lonely and dreary,
The days when Thou hidest Thy face;
How sorrow and sadness
Are turned into gladness,
By a glimpse of its love and its grace.

Come nearer, come nearer,
And make Thyself dearer,
Thou joy, Thou delight of my heart!
Close, close to Thee pressing
I long for Thy blessing,
I cannot without it depart.

SORROW

I.

I have known Sorrow; I have been acquainted
  With her pale face; her voice, her footstep known;
Oft uninvited she has crossed my threshold,
    To speak with me alone.

II.

I loved her not! I gave to her no welcome;
  Asked not her errand, closed to her my heart;
With chilling words, and with a face averted,
    I urged her to depart.

III.

She went, but came again; as a dove flutters
  About some dear retreat, she oft returned;
I heard her wings but offered her no shelter,
    Her coming flight I spurned.

IV.

At last, by my repelling frowns unwearied,
  Again she ventured nigh, and thus she spake:
"I come from One thou lovest!" showed her tokens,
    Grew welcome, for His sake.

V.

Thenceforth she sat my guest, revered and honored.
  And her stern face unlovely ceased to be.
When life interpreting, she sat beside me,
    Made Christ more dear to me.

VI.

And yet her presence drove from out my threshold,
  The treasures that His hand in bounty gave;
Groans wrung she from me, as I knelt in anguish
    At the relentless grave.

VII.

Upon the rock of sore suspense she laid me,
  Not once, but often, tore me limb from limb;

And when I shrank, and wept, and cried for mercy,
   She pointed but to Him.

VIII.

And so by turns sore-smitten, soothed, instructed,
   I sit at her dear feet, and smile on her,
Who came on wings of love to scourge and prove me—
   Christ's precious messenger!

"GOD LOVES TO BE LONGED FOR, HE LOVES TO BE SOUGHT"

Lord, is this true? Ah, canst Thou really love
  These longings in the soul, that only tell
Of emptiness, of depths unsatisfied,
  Of waves that on a boundless ocean swell?

And dost Thou love me when I only seek,
  Yet do not find Thee? When I go astray,
And stumble blindly onward in the dark,
  And cannot see, but only feel, my way?

Ah! I am truly longing! Both my arms
  Are stretched, with speechless yearnings, after Thee;
Naught else have I to give Thee, dearest Lord,
  No grace, no beauty, canst Thou see in me.

And I am truly seeking! All day long,
  In silent thought and prayer, to Thee I turn;
At home, abroad, alone, or in the crowd,
  I strive to find Thee, strive Thy paths to learn.

Longing and seeking! These two words declare
  All that I am and hope for; great the thought
That Thou canst love this longing, love the heart
  That, while it seeks Thee, in itself is naught.

Jesus, dear Master, give to me the power
  Thy name to love, to honor and adore;
I long for Thee! I seek Thee! Let me long,
  And let me ever seek Thee, more and more.

BROKEN TO BE MENDED

Suggested by the remark of a bereaved friend:
"We cannot be mended unless we are broken."

Jesus, our tears with blessed smiles are blending,
 For Thou who knowest how our hearts to break,
Knowest the happy secret of their mending,
 And we rejoice in sorrow for Thy sake.

Yes, break us all to pieces, at Thy pleasure,
 For the poor fragments can be joined by Thee;
Snatch from us, if Thou wilt, our every treasure!
 Possessing Thee we never poor can be.

There is a sweetness in a spirit broken,
 That lofty souls attain not—cannot know;
To such a heart Thy promises are spoken,[1]
 Thou hast a solace for its silent woe.

And when our weary days on earth are ended,
 And from its agitations we are free,
We shall rejoice that we were broken, mended,
 By Thine own skillful hand, dear Lord, by Thee!

---

1 Psalm 51:17—The sacrifices of God are a broken spirit: a
broken and a contrite heart, O God, thou wilt not despise.

"THAT I MAY WIN CHRIST"

Dear Jesus, every morning's light
  Brings a new love to Thee;
Each makes of Thee a new delight,
  New strength, new joy to me.

I want to give myself away
  In bonds as fresh, as new;
Let a new love be born each day,
  A love more deep, more true.

I would forget, in pressing on,
  All that is left behind.
A changeless goal has not been won,
  Not yet my Lord I find.

The goal is changing! With each morn
  There springs a higher aim,
With each are deeper longings born,
  Life's object not the same.

Thou dost, with Thine inspiring grace,
  My halting steps allure;
I know that I shall see Thy face,
  To win Thee I am sure.

Oh, who, such blessed race to run,
  Would not each morning rise,
Knowing that God's eternal Son
  Shall be the victor's prize?

AN ANGEL SMILING

Dear Lord, into my heart, already sore,
　Sharp, piercing thorns are pressing;
I recognize the Hand that oft before,
　Has, in such guise, sent blessing.

I shrink not from this pain; my hands clasp Thine
　To help it pierce the deeper;
I know these wounds are precious and divine,
　I am a happy weeper.

For oh! I weep not that I smart and bleed,
　But that my patient willing,
Falls in with Thy dear will in thought and deed,
　And every pain is stilling.

I weep because Thy will has grown so sweet,
　That even a thorn brings gladness;
That all which humbles, drives me to Thy feet,
　Is precious sadness.

So pierce, so wound, my Master, for this heart
　Against Thy thorns is pressing,
Rejoicing in their pain, and in their smart,
　Thy tenderness confessing.

Oh, blessed Will of God! It sorrow daunts
　While of its sting beguiling;
And where a torment only stood, it plants
　An angel smiling.

YEARNING

How long it is since I have seen Thy face,
　　And how I yearn to see it! Dearest Lord,
I dare not ask to see it, though such grace
　　Transporting joy and gladness would afford.

Let me be patient in this long delay;
　　If I have lost Thee, all the fault is mine—
Perhaps when Thou wert near I turned away—
　　And lost the light that would upon me shine.

Forgive the folly, and forgive the sin—
　　It was not wilful,—how it came and when,—
At what vile door the Tempter entered in,
　　I do not know: oh turn him out again.

For I am very weary, very sad—
　　Life is so desolate afar from Thee;
I miss the joys sublime that once I had;
　　I long, I yearn for Thy lost sympathy.

THE CHRISTIAN LIFE

Wouldst thou take the gauge of the Christian life,
 And measure it out by rule?
Wouldst thou circumscribe it, and plane it down,
 And define it in some school?

But there is no plummet can reach its depths;
 No foot that can scale its heights;
No painter its varying features paint,
 No poet its pure delights.

Its mystical grace is grace of its own,
 And springs from a mystic Fount;
Now in the valley it makes its way,
 And now it ascends the mount.

Believe in it, trust it, with all thy soul,
 And love it with all thine heart;
Seek it where others have sought it out,
 And learn what they can impart.

But he who knows, and who loves it best,
 Will ever declare to thee,
It is all a wonder, a miracle,
 And always a mystery!

HE IS MINE

I.

O Christ, I yearn for more of Thee;
Reveal, reveal Thyself to me,
    And satisfy this heart
    That would be Thine alone.
I want Thee wholly, not in part,
I want to know that mine Thou art,
    To know as I am known;
Within this breast Thy love has glowed,
Oh, come and make it Thine abode.

II.

When I can see Thy face divine,
A sunbeam seems on me to shine;
    And if Thou turn away,
    Joy ceases to be joy.
Night's blackest darkness stifles day,
I am of restless grief the prey,
    Its idle sport and toy;
I know, for I have tasted this—
Have missed Thee, mourned Thee, felt Thy bliss.

III.

Oh, Thou my Life, my Joy, my End,
Dearer than any earthly friend,
    How can I speak Thy love?
    What say I have not said?
When streaming eyes have looked above,
These hands held fast the heavenly Dove,
    That pleaded in my stead:
Has not Thy penetrating glance
Read that which knows no utterance?

IV.

And yet I yearn to love Thee more,
With saintly rapture to adore
    Thy dear and precious Name,

That must be dearer yet;
I come Thy promises to claim,
Thy love my boldness will not blame,
 Thy heart my plea forget;
Let praises be my every breath,
My hourly life of self the death.

V.

Thou hast lit up with ardor rare
Some hidden souls, Thy special care;
 Make me to them akin!
 Give me what Thou to them hast given,
Their high devotion let me win,
Their calm dominion over sin,
 Making of earth a heaven—
The wondrous and mysterious grace
Of ever looking on Thy face!

VI.

They went to meet Thee by a way
That pilgrim feet still tread today,
 And counting all things dross
 Save Him they in long patience sought;
Let me press on through pain and loss,
Bending beneath my Master's cross,
 Learning as they were taught;
Jesus, Beloved of my heart,
I feel Thine answer—mine Thou art!

"AM I MY BROTHER'S KEEPER?"

Am I my brother's keeper? Yes,
    I owe him love and care;
The word of counsel and of cheer;
    The power of earnest prayer.

When fierce temptation shakes his soul,
    My strength should be his stay;
When flattering voices lure to sin,
    My form should bar his way.

When sickness lays him low, my time,
    My faithful ministries,
My health, my courage, all I have,
    Should patiently be his.

And when his day of life grows dark,
    And tears his eye bedim,
Mine is the heart to feel his grief,
    To sympathize with him.

My brother's keeper, then, am I;
    O Christ, within me shine,
That mine may be the sacred joy
    To help him to be Thine.

ALONE WITH GOD

Into my closet fleeing, as the dove
    Doth homeward flee,
I haste away to ponder o'er Thy love
    Alone with Thee!

In the dim wood, by human ear unheard,
    Joyous and free,
Lord! I adore Thee, feasting on Thy word
    Alone with Thee!

Amid the busy city, thronged and gay,
    But One I see,
Tasting sweet peace, as unobserved I pray
    Alone with Thee!

Oh happy life! Life hid with Christ in God!
    So making me,
At home, and by the wayside, and abroad,
    Alone with Thee!

IT CANNOT LAST

Weary now it is, and must be,
 All my sky is overcast;
But no cloud can be eternal,
 This one cannot always last!

Drearily the storm is beating,
 Chilling rain is falling fast;
I am wet, and cold, and cheerless;
 But it cannot always last!

Walls of granite, stern, forbidding,
 Separate me from the past,
That was erst so glad, so joyous;—
 But they cannot always last!

And what sorrows lie before me
 In the future drear and vast;
Ah, I know not! But it cheers me
 That they cannot always last!

SOMETHING FOR CHRIST

Something for Thee! Lord, let this be
   Thy choice for me from day to day;
The life I live it is not mine,
Thy will, my will, have made it Thine!
   Oh let me do in Thine own way,
     Something for Thee!

Something for Thee! What shall it be?
   Speak, Lord, Thy waiting servant hears,
Is it to do some mighty deed?
Is it some multitude to feed?
   Is it to do mid pains and fears,
     Something for Thee?

Something for Thee! I do not see
   A coming battle for my King;
I only see a little cup—
With water haste to fill it up:
   Thy love will own this trivial thing,
     Something for Thee!

Something for Thee! From self I flee,
   What wilt Thou, Master, from me still?
With eager heart I stand and wait,
Longing for work, or small or great:
   Let me be doing as Thy will,
     Something for Thee!

Something for Thee! On bended knee,
   Unseen, unknown by mortal eye,
My soul for other souls shall plead—
As Thou for me didst intercede.
   Thy love can own a tear, a sigh,
     Something for Thee!

Something for Thee! Yet if for me
   It is a useless, crippled hand,
Let perfect patience mark my way:

Since they who silently obey
Are doing as Thy wisdom planned,
Something for Thee!

FORGIVE!

Dear Lord, forgive
The evil passions that within me live,
Make my whole heart
Of Thine a part,
And let Thy Spirit rule and reign in me
That I may perfect be, complete in Thee.

I do hate sin
And all the wretched work it does within;
I cannot rest,
When in my breast,
I see its motions and its mad desires,
Oh purge me, Lord, e'en though it be through fires.

THE PILGRIM

From the German of Schiller.
Read this poem of Schiller's with that Name, which is above every name,
as its solution. "The there" is "here."—Mrs. Charles.

Life was only in its spring-tide,
　　When to wander forth inclined,
Youth I left with all its gladness
　　In my father's house behind.

Joyful, full of faith, my birthright,
　　All I had I tossed away,
Then a pilgrim's staff inclasping,
　　Childish folly won the day.

For a mighty hope inspired me,
　　Faith clasped hands with vague desire:
"On," I cried, "the way is open,
　　Ever upward, ever higher!

"On, until a golden portal
　　Shall to enter welcome thee;
There the earthly shall be heavenly,
　　Heavenly and immortal be."

It was night, and came the morning,
　　Never, never stood I still;
But there yet remained concealed
　　What I wanted, what would will.

Mountains rose to bar my progress,
　　Rivers deep my way withstood,
Over gulfs I built me causeways,
　　Passed in safety, bridged the flood.

To a river's shore arriving,
　　Whose wide current eastward prest,
Full of faith, I gladly cast me
　　Straight into its flowing breast.

Making me its sport, it bore me
　　Onward to a mighty sea:

Naught but empty space before me,
   All I aimed for fled from me.

Ah! no bridge will lead me thither;
   Heaven will not to earth come near,
But forever smile beyond me,
   While the *There* is never *Here.*

WORK

Lord, what would'st Thou have me to do?

Lord, send me work to do for Thee,
    Let not a single day
Be spent in waiting on myself,
    Or wasted pass away.

And teach me how to work for Thee;
    Thy Spirit, Lord, impart,
That I may serve Thee less from fear
    Than from a loving heart.

And bless the work I do for Thee,
    Or I shall toil in vain;
Mine be the hand to drop the seed;
    Thine to send sun and rain.

Thrice happy he who works for Thee;
    Thou grantest him the grace,
When he takes home his work to see
    The Master, face to face.

JESUS, BE ALL

O Lord, I know that Thou wilt give to me
    All that I really want;
And yet with heart insatiate and athirst
    For more of Thee I pant.

Bid me long on: help me to strive and pray,
    For I would rather kneel
Rent by conflicting wants, than never thirst
    For Thee, my Lord, to feel.

Give me the prayer of faith, that must prevail!
    Dictate what my poor heart
Shall say to Thee, and how it shall be said,
    Jesus, till mine Thou art.

Come to me with my earliest waking thought,
    Be with me where I go;
Be my last thought at night, and in my dreams
    Thy blessed presence show.

I am so weak, so helpless, Thou so strong;
    Oh, do not let me fall!
My self-despair alone must plead my cause;
    Jesus, be Thou mine all!

COMPLETE IN CHRIST

"Ye are complete in Him."

Complete in Him! Oh, Lord, I flee,
Laden with this great thought, to Thee;
With tears and smiles contending, cry,
Are words like these for such as I?

Complete in Him! No word of mine
Is needed, Lord, to perfect Thine;
Wise Master-Builder, let Thy hand
Fashion the fabric Thou hast planned.

Complete in Him! I nothing bring,
Am an imperfect, useless thing;
But human eyes shall joy to see
What God's dear hand shall add to me.

Complete in Him! Oh, longed-for day,
When my poor, sinful heart can say,
Naught in myself, for ruin meet,
In Jesus Christ I stand complete!

"JOY UNSPEAKABLE"

I.

The Christian life! What is its explanation?
　　Is it a law of discipline and pain?
So stern a law that hearts can never carol
　　A cheerful, gladsome strain?

II.

Is it set only to a cadence mournful?
　　A Miserere its peculiar song?
Surely we ever hear it, often vainly
　　For Jubilates long.

III.

Man's grief is sacred, yet he sometimes tells it
　　But of his deeper joy he cannot speak;
He struggles in its mystery, and to paint it
　　Finds human words too weak.

IV.

The shallow brook, that its own way is taking,
　　Sings songs incessant, as it onward goes;
It has no depths, no waves, no hidden secrets;
　　It has no ebbs and flows.

V.

We hear the ocean moaning, sighing ever,
　　We hear its restless tossings and its roar;
But of the "central peace" within its bosom,
　　It never tells us more.

VI.

Like it, majestic, human joy is speechless;
　　Like it, yet more, the joy divine is mute;
"Speech" may be "silvern," but a "golden silence"
　　Is rapture's attribute.

VII.

Look for the soul whose glance is ever upward,
　　Who sees the living Christ, who knows the grace

Of His mysterious friendship; loves Him, trusts Him;
  Speaks to Him, face to face:

VIII.

And you have found a soul, that though it utter
  Ofttimes a groan, and ofttimes sheds a tear,
Knows of a bliss whose language is transcendent,
  And cannot reach the ear.

IX.

Thrice blessed soul! It cannot tell its story—
  Cannot, to mortal ear, its depths betray;
But it shall tell it, giving Christ the glory,
  In His effulgent Day!

THE CRY OF THE YOUNG WIFE

I.

What o'clock is it, Nurse? Just one? Why, I thought it was four;
That must be moonlight, then, lying so white on the floor.
Ah, what long nights! And I have not been sleeping at all,
But lying here watching your shadow nod this way and that, on the wall.

II.

Wet my lips, Nurse; give me drink; put some ice to my head;
No, not there—here on my forehead! oh, how you're shaking the bed!
Oh, that I lay like the moonlight so cold and so white,
But I'm burning with fever, and tired, so tired tonight!

III.

In the morning I sigh for the evening; at night I pine for the day.
All my young life-blood is scorching and drying away.
Well, let it dry! For my life it is nothing to me,
At best 'tis a fetter, and I only long to be free.

IV.

The child, do you say? Nay, don't talk to me of the child!
Lay more ice on my forehead; be quiet, and don't look so wild.
Best for the stream at its fountain to fail and to dry,
Best for the child with its young little mother to die.

V.

For I am so young! I'm so young! Oh, Nurse, don't you know
What a happy young creature I was only four weeks ago?
He called me his darling, his plaything, his baby—but nay,
I'm his widow—do you hear? I am his widow, today.

VI.

I always thought widows were old; wore stiff caps and gray curls;
Never dreamed that they ever were made of young girls!
But I'm a young girl, and my Philip was only a boy—
Brilliant and handsome. Why, just to behold him was joy!

VII.

Why did I let him go forth to that terrible fight?
They say it was all for his country; that he died for the triumph of right.

Well, let the country rejoice. It has snatched my love from my side,
And made me a widow when I was scarcely a bride.

VIII.

Do you say it's the fever that makes all my talking so wild?
That, perhaps, I could cry and get eased if I would but look at my child?
Nay, nothing can give me ease now till my hands you enfold,
And lay me down under the moonlight, as white and as cold.

THE SONG OF THE YOUNG MOTHER

IX.

Ah, my own baby! I love thee, I love thee at last!
The tempest of sorrow is over, the night of my anguish is past!
Come to my heart, thou bright creature! closer, ah, closer, my boy!
The world it no longer is empty, it is brimming, is brimming with joy!

X.

Ah, my own baby! My darling! Thy father's own glorious child!
Radiant in beauty thou art, and, like him, undefiled;
All the mad love that I gave him I pour out on thee;
The world it no longer is empty; but the fullness of fullness to me!

Sings—We'll grow up together, my baby,
  Thou and I together;
 We'll go hopping from bough to bough,
  Little birds of a feather!
   And we will play
   In fragrant hay,
   And berries sweet
   Together eat;
 Thou'lt forget I'm thy little mother—
 I'll make believe thou'rt my little brother!
 Thou shalt be all in all to me;
 I will be all in all to thee.
 And, by-and-by, when thou art a man,
 I'll be just as young as I can;

Never maiden, never a bride,
Shall steal my darling away from my side;
A soldier's death thou shalt never die,
In a soldier's grave thou shalt never lie;
But gay and joyful thy life shall be,
Thou shalt be all in all to me,
And I will be all in all to thee!

HER SIGH

XI.

Down 'mid high grass a mother-bird built her a nest;
I was that bird; and my nestling it lies there at rest!
Was it long years ago—was it but yesterday, say?
That laying him down there I left him, and went on my way?

XII.

Sorrow has sought me and found me; sorrow has silvered my hair;
At my table he sits my sole guest; facing me solemnly there;
He has stolen my youth and my laughter; stolen my life and my joy,
Snatched away husband and lover, seized on my beautiful boy.

XIII.

Ah, I was joyous and thoughtless; evil and danger defied,
Forth from gay childhood I ran to the life of a bride.
I must have something to love; on something must pour out my heart:
Little recked I of trouble, little of thorn and of smart.

XIV.

And then they must kill him, my husband, my lover, my all!
Shivered in fragments my heart with the same fatal ball!
Shivered in fragments, and frozen and lifeless it lay,
Whose were the hands that its warmth to restore could assay!

XV.

Thine, my own baby! None other! Ah, the first wakings to joy,
Under the touch of thy fingers, my darling, my beautiful boy!
Green grew the earth 'neath my feet, blue the sky over my head!
Of one idol bereft, in my heart I enthroned thee instead.

XVI.

So the new current of life went babbling along,
Sparkling and gleesome, and full of its youth and its song;
We had not a moment for sadness, never a moment to sigh,
We were two children together, just my own baby and I!

HER NEW SONG

Dear Lord, my heart was but a willful thing,
Strong in its strength and ever on the wing:
It needed mastership, and Thou hast claimed it,
It needed taming, and Thy hand has tamed it.
Now, gentle, peaceful, harmless as a dove,
It lives as erst it lived its life, in love;
Love to all living things that Thou hast made;
A love that is all sunshine without shade.
Thy fair, green earth is dotted as with flowers,
With little human souls, and blissful hours
I spend in blessed ministries to them.
Ah, many a flower I gather, many a gem!
And I have Thee! No battle's rude affray
Can ever tear Thee from my heart away;
And the cold hand that stole my boy from me,
Can never lay a claiming touch on Thee!
And so my life goes on, and to some eyes
Flinty and lonely all my pathway lies;
But Thou, who taking much, so much hast given,
Hast granted me the very peace of Heaven.
Through loss I passed to gain! Through death to life!
I kiss the rod that smote the youthful wife,
And love Him best who took away the boy,
And woke the mother from her dream of joy.
My God, Thine eye, omniscient and divine,
Rests on no happier, gladder heart than mine;
Empty of all things else, what room for Thee,
Who hast been, art, and will be, All to me!

APPENDIX

"NEW YEAR THOUGHTS"

From "The Sabbath at Home."

Those who read the beautiful lines thus entitled in the January number of this Magazine, will feel that a touching and sacred interest is attached to them when they learn that the warm heart that dictated, and the hand that gave them language, then lay cold in death.

Their author, Mrs. JULIA B. CADY, was young and happy; the joy and pride of a sweet, Christian home; a blessed wife and mother, with everything to attract her to this life. But her face was ever set right heavenward; and when, just as the old year was closing, the summons to come up higher reached her, she had nothing to do but to lay aside her earthly garments, and to go. She had lived for Christ: her time, her thoughts, her work were all for him. She loved His poor for His sake, and gathered them about her, counseled them, prayed with them, found employment for them, made herself one with them. She loved to welcome friendless waifs, tossed upon the tide of this great sea of city life, into hospitable shelter. She loved little children, and made their interests her own. She loved the Church of Christ, and, one sacramental season after another, saw those united to it whose feet she had guided there. In a word, she loved Christ, and walked with God in an unobtrusive and meek pathway, that has now led her straight to his eternal embrace.

And hardly had she gone hence, when, like a voice from the grave, there came to her astonished, weeping friends, who saw it now for the first time, this cheerful greeting to the New Year; precious words, reserved for their joy and solace when they should enter that year without her. Would there were more homes like hers! Would there were more souls as saintly, as rich in faith and love, as hers! Would that every one who reads this brief notice could face the unknown future with the calm confidence with which she confronted it!

One touching incident may, perhaps, be added. At the close of the funeral-services, two friends stole back to the church to take one more look at the peaceful face. There she lay, amid an opulent— nay, a regal profusion of flowers, the gift of those who had loved and honored her and hers; and a group of poor women and children hung around her coffin, giving all they had to give. It was a beautiful contrast, such as is rarely seen upon earth; the testimony of the rich and the testimony of the poor—the flowers of the one, and the tears of the other. How little she knew, when she asked the coming year what it had in store for her, that it had these flowers and these tears, and the "Well done, good and faithful servant! enter into the joy of thy Lord!"

NEW YEAR THOUGHTS

Farewell, Old Year! the rustle of whose garment,
　　Fragrant with memory, I still can hear:
For all thy tender kindness and thy bounty
　　I drop my thankful tribute on thy bier.

What is in store for me, brave New Year, hidden
　　Beneath thy glistening robe of ice and snows?
Are there sweet songs of birds, and breath of lilacs,
　　And blushing blooms of June's scent-laden rose?

Are there cold winds and dropping leaves of autumn,
　　Heart-searching frosts, and storm-clouds black and drear?
Is there a rainbow spanning the dark heaven?
　　Wilt thou not speak and tell me, glad New Year?

As silent art thou of the unknown future
　　As if thy days were numbered with the dead;
Yet, as I enter thy wide-open portal,
　　I cross thy threshold with glad hope, not dread.

To me no pain or fear or crushing sorrow
　　Hast thou the power without *His* will to bring;
And so I fear thee not, O untried morrow!
　　For well I know my *Father* is thy King.

If joy thou bringest, straight to God, the giver,
　　My gratitude shall rise; for 'tis his gift:
If sorrow, still, 'mid waves of Grief's deep river,
　　My trembling heart I'll to my Father lift.

If life's full cup shall be my happy potion,
 With thankful joy I'll drink the precious draught;
If death, my waiting soul across Life's ocean
 But little sooner to my home 'twill waft.

So hope-lit New Year, with thy joys uncertain,
 Whose unsolved mystery none may foretell,
I calmly trust my God to lift thy curtain:
 Safe in his love, for *me* 'twill all be well.

JULIA B. CADY

REPLY OF THE NEW YEAR

What had I hidden for thee in my bosom,
    Thou fearless listener at my closed door?
With what sweet songs was I prepared to greet thee?
    What were the fragrant flowers I held in store?

Was it the song of birds, the breath of lilacs,
    The blushing blooms of June's scent-laden rose,
The rainbow-hues of beauty and of promise,
    The cup that with life's gladness overflows?

Nay, thou beloved one! Songs of angel voices
    Are the sweet notes that waited for thine ear;
Immortal are the flowers my hands had gathered
    To deck thy pathway to the brave New Year.

Mine was the joy to clasp thy hand, and lead thee
    Into green pastures: guide thy willing feet,
That oft had strayed that way, to the full fountain,
    To crystal rivers, waters clear and sweet;

To see thee in the garments pure and spotless
    In which His loved ones are by Jesus dressed;
Behold thee take possession of the mansion
    Provided for the long-expected guest.

Farewell, thou missed and mourned! In those fair regions,
    Where now thou art at home, there are no years;
There are no pains, or fears, or crushing sorrows,
    No frosts, no storm clouds, no cold winds, no tears.

Thine is no doubtful path, no fate uncertain;
    For thee no anxious fear one heart may swell:
But tear-dimmed eyes pierce Death's transparent curtain,
    And see thee safe with Christ,—all well, all well!

January 3, 1870.

www.ingramcontent.com/pod-product-compliance
Lightning Source LLC
Chambersburg PA
CBHW070837100426
42813CB00003B/649